About the author

Dave Robinson taught philosophy for many years. He has also written quite a lot of books about individual philosophers and philosophical subjects, including the graphic guides *Introducing Ethics* and *Introducing Philosophy* (both published by Icon). These days he spends most of his time walking, growing vegetables, painting landscapes and arguing with his friends. He is learning to play the ukulele in the privacy of his garden shed. He tries to follow some of the advice in this book.

Contents

Introduction:
asking questions

Drifting or thinking?

Most of us drift through life without asking difficult questions. We're not very interested in what knowledge is, or about what is real, or whether you can ever find the answers to moral problems. But philosophers are restless. They can't stop asking questions, even though the answers are often hard to find. They examine very odd problems like 'What is reality?' or 'What is a good person?' They are like children in a way – impossibly curious, sometimes about what seems totally obvious. ('What is real?' 'Are you having a laugh?')

The first great philosopher was Socrates, and he insisted that everyone had to think for themselves. He said it's important not to believe everything that other people tell you. Life is usually easier if you go along with everybody else, but it's lazy. We all need to think for ourselves. It's one of the things that makes us fully human. Socrates asked awkward questions and was eventually killed for voicing his opinions. Everyone now admires him for sticking to his beliefs. So part of being a good person means not 'obeying the rules' but 'thinking for yourself'.

Do philosophers have the answers?

Nobody is quite sure what philosophy is these days, especially philosophers. Some say it tries to answer the questions that science has given up on. What are these questions that baffle science?

THINK ABOUT IT

A scientist can tell you what 'stem cell research' means and how it might help sick people, but he can't tell you, for sure, whether it's right or wrong. A philosopher can examine a moral problem like this in detail and make suggestions. But, at the end of the day, she can't tell you the 'moral truth' either.

You have to decide for yourself whether stem cell research is right or wrong, *in your opinion*. Notice those last three words. No one can prove that stem cell research is good or bad. You can only ever have opinions.

That doesn't mean we can't make very confident guesses or have strong moral views. It's just that philosophers will always want to know **how** you know. Some of us will say that we rely on something we call our 'conscience' – but what's that? Some rely on others – parents, 'experts', or the man next door. Some of us may have firm moral views already, because we've been taught them in church or at the mosque. But philosophers aren't happy with 'Someone told me' or 'I read it in the Great Book'. They want reasons, evidence, a logical argument.

Changing morality

Morality gets passed down from generation to generation without being questioned much. But it can change. At one time most people thought that there was nothing wrong in watching a bear being ripped to pieces by a pack of dogs. It made a splendid day out for all the family. Nowadays we're more alarmed and distressed by needless cruelty to animals and we think that bear-baiting was wrong. A lot of us now think that fox hunting is probably cruel as well. And most people no longer think that homosexuality is wicked. It looks as if society has progressed. But we shouldn't be too smug. Human beings aren't necessarily getting nicer, year on year. We still do bad things. And new moral problems keep surfacing that we don't know how to deal with. Should we allow the government to lock people up without trial, in case they are terrorists? Should we allow them to torture suspects to find out more information?

Sometimes wrong and always wrong

So why do moral beliefs change like this? Where do they come from in the first place? The easy answer to that one is 'society'. Societies can be very different. They can change. The moral beliefs of medieval Japan are very different from those of modern America. Slavery was quite acceptable 200 years ago. So was slavery right then and wrong now, or has it always been wrong? Is there always one obviously right thing to do, regardless of when or where you live?

Some philosophers called **absolutists** would say yes, slavery has always been wrong, regardless of what people once believed. **Relativists** say no, moral beliefs are always relative – slavery was 'right' at one time but now it's 'wrong'.

And people still disagree about some moral issues. Everyone agrees that attacking a poor old woman and stealing her pension is wrong. No one would argue about that. But people still debate other more complex problems like abortion and animal experiments, and it's sometimes hard for us to know who to agree with. A lot of moral problems can be very difficult to puzzle out.

The uses of philosophy

This is where **moral philosophy** can be very useful. It won't tell you what to think. It won't give you a set of rules to be obeyed at all times, without question. But it will help you to puzzle things out. Philosophy examines what lies behind our moral judgements. It attempts to explain what a 'good person' is like.

Using the ideas of moral philosophy and practical, real-life situations, this book will help you to make up your mind about the moral problems you're likely to face in everyday life. Philosophy can't guarantee that you will always make the correct ethical decision, but it will give you a better understanding of how and why you decided as you did.

Here are a few moral questions (**Q**) to get you started, along with some responses (**R**). (N.B. These are 'responses' and not 'answers', because moral statements are firm *beliefs*, reinforced with evidence and convincing arguments. There are no rigid *answers*.)

Q At one time, no one thought there was anything wrong with slavery. Now we think it's wrong. Why do we? Why did slave owners think it was OK?

R Slavery is and always was wrong. (IMHO, as they say on Facebook – in my humble opinion.) How can a human being ever be someone else's 'property'? Every individual has the right to be free and treated with dignity. Slave owners themselves didn't like to think too much about the ethics of slavery. They came up with ridiculous excuses to justify what they were doing. Aristotle said that slaves were slaves 'by nature', whatever that means.

Q Are there any moral rules that you think are always non-negotiable and compulsory? What are they?

R Torture of any kind is always wrong and never justified (IMHO). Being cruel to children is too. You can probably think of a few more.

Q What would you need to do before you said, 'Stem cell research is wicked'?

R Whatever moral issue you feel strongly about, like stem cell research, make sure that you know all the facts first, and think hard about it. Don't just say, 'It's wrong because it's wrong'.

Q Which of these moral issues do you feel most strongly about? (Mark them from 1 to 10.)

Abortion
Animal rights
Bankers' greed
Global warming
Euthanasia

R This ranking of moral issues is *your own*. It might tell you some interesting things about your personal moral beliefs.

Q Where do you think your moral beliefs come from? Your parents? Your friends? TV and newspapers? Your conscience? Somewhere else?

R Moral beliefs come from all over the place. Everyone is influenced by different things. Your parents tell you the basics – don't lie, steal or be cruel. Newspapers and TV are usually good sources of information but may be suspect when it comes to moral pronouncements. At the end of the day, you have to think for yourself and then decide.

Q An ancient tribe in New Guinea practises cannibalism enthusiastically. They believe that when they eat a grandfather, or an enemy slain in battle, they are also ingesting the strength, wisdom and courage of these people. Should we intervene and stop them?

R Do we stop other people's cultural practices? Personally I can't see anything wrong about eating a grandfather who died of natural causes, although I wouldn't want to do it myself. I'm less happy about eating defeated enemies. I might try to encourage this tribe to settle boundary disputes in a less aggressive way. As a sophisticated modern European who has read some anthropology and sociology, I would always be reluctant to impose my own morality and etiquette onto others. So in this case I'm a relativist. It's their morality, not mine. But if they also went in for compulsory widow-burning, then I would try to stop them. Burning people against their will just seems wrong to me – always. So in that instance I'm an absolutist. Who said morality was easy?

CASE STUDY

I met Matt down at the pub and he was furious. What was the problem? Apparently his employer had suggested that all his employees donate 2 per cent of their wages to a Third World charity. Matt thinks he's worked hard all week and deserves all of his pay. Why should he give £6 a week to help people he's never even met? What has any of this got to do with him? Charity begins at home, he says. Whose side are you on? Matt's? Or his employer's?

The philosopher Peter Singer (b. 1946) says that if Matt saw a starving child lying on the pavement outside the pub, then he'd feel morally obliged to give him money for a meal and tell the authorities about him. But there are thousands of starving children in Africa and elsewhere. Just because Matt can't see them doesn't mean he shouldn't have to think about helping them. Does geographical distance make them less worthy of help?

And it's not as if £6 is a huge amount out of £300. What Matt seems to be objecting to more is his loss of **autonomy** – his own freedom to choose, and he's right that no one should be forced to donate money to charity. Matt has to make a personal decision.

1. Moral philosophy: a very rough history

At the very beginning

So when did moral philosophy begin? Codes of behaviour have always existed, ever since human beings started living together to hunt, forage, grow crops and keep domestic animals. Tribal chiefs and priests insisted that individuals abstained from anti-social activities like murder and theft. These things are called 'anti-social' because no society can get off the ground if they are widespread. It's impossible to keep tribes, cities or societies intact if there's a moral free-for-all.

So, on the whole, people carried on believing what their parents believed. Everyone frowned on unorthodox views or unusual behaviour. Nothing much changed. There was no such thing as 'modern'. You used the same tools, built the same huts and pyramids, went through the usual 'reaching puberty' rituals, married, had kids, taught them what you'd been taught, and so it went on for thousands of years. Technology changed – flint tools got replaced by bronze and then iron ones – but most people still distrusted ethical or political innovation. Anyone who challenged orthodox moral or religious beliefs got laughed at or severely punished. Morality, religion and politics were all interwoven into one unavoidable system. No one ever thought to ask where moral rules came from or why they had to be obeyed. They were usually just too tired or frightened.

The Greeks: thinking new thoughts

Then the ancient Greeks arrived. To begin with, they were warrior tribes who fought each other and laid siege to cities. They admired courage and military heroes, celebrated in the works of Homer such as the *Iliad* and the *Odyssey*. But then one lot of Greeks, the citizens of Athens, became more modern, more like us. Athens was unusual in that it began to be ruled by direct democracy, which meant that all adult males were voters and members of the government. Slaves did the hard work like farming, mining, metalworking, making pots and furniture, writing letters and teaching children, so Athenian citizens had lots of free time on their hands. They went to religious festivals, plays and athletic competitions, and gave dinner parties.

All of this leisure also meant that some individuals had the time and opportunity to think for themselves instead of just going along with tradition. Greek gods and goddesses were venerated and feared but often behaved quite badly, punishing human beings out of sexual jealousy, for instance. So Athenians couldn't look to their religion for moral instruction. This meant that they started to ask strange questions about morality and other things like mathematics, science, astronomy and politics. And it's this that makes them more like us. They asked questions about the rest of the world and the universe, as well as about their own lives.

KEY FIGURE The first really famous Athenian moral philosopher was Socrates (469–399 BC). He was poor but proud. He seems to have made a living as a stonemason and he always refused to charge for philosophical advice. He was a very charismatic character who attracted many young followers. One of them was Plato, who wrote down everything we know about him. Socrates insisted that we must always argue and debate with each other – that way we usually find that we don't really know what we've been talking about! And he was a rather odd sort of 'guru' because he always insisted that he knew nothing himself. He thought that you should constantly examine your prejudices, beliefs, worries and anxieties. 'The unexamined life is not worth living', he said.

Socrates is right, of course. We are all driven by motives, feelings and prejudices that we rarely question. Modern Westerners like us still tend to believe that the consumption and ownership of 'things' will make us happier. It's probably a wrong belief. We all have ideas that are 'manufactured' by others whose interests have more to do with their profit than our well-being. Our modern world is changing fast, and we have to adapt to it, get used to new gadgets, vocabulary, ideas, needs and wants – at speed. Socrates would say that we should take time out to examine our beliefs. What are the things that are really important to us?

The philosophy of ethics was begun by this snub-nosed, hen-pecked old Athenian who always insisted that we're more ignorant than we realize – especially about behaving well.

Knowing and choosing

Unfortunately Socrates concluded that behaving morally came from knowing what is 'good' – which makes wickedness just a kind of ignorance. The difference between the good man and the villain is that the good one is more informed. But what's wrong with this idea? Look at the example below.

THINK ABOUT IT

The Kray brothers set up extensive protection rackets, which they ran with ruthless efficiency. They injured people and murdered them. They did this because they were ignorant of the moral rules forbidding extortion and violence. They were wicked because they were stupid.

This isn't right, is it? Socrates seems to have got something badly wrong here. The Krays knew what they did was wrong, all right. They weren't ignorant or stupid, just bad. So it looks as if being moral involves **choosing** to do good things as well as **knowing** what they are.

Freedom and choice

Being a good person in our modern world isn't easy. We don't live in small city states like Athens. Most of us live in a 'liberal' democracy.

Liberalism is a way of thinking about governments and individual citizens. It says that governments are limited in what they can do. They can pass laws to protect our freedom and property, but they can't force us to be 'good' people. Citizens are 'free' because governments can't interfere with our private lives.

Liberals assume that human beings are mostly selfish anyway – interested only in their own wealth and happiness. This is partly because we live in a capitalist society or 'market' now, where everyone is competing against everyone else. It's like a race – we all begin equally, the brightest and most energetic do best and the stupid and lazy do worst. That's what life is all about. So it's fair. What do you think about that?

Liberalism and capitalism have both been very successful, especially in the developed world. We're all wealthier now and we're relatively free. We can choose. But liberalism has no game-plan, except for more of the same – bigger supermarkets and more 'choice' for everyone. Nowadays we all live private lives and have little sense of community any more. Many of us don't even know who our immediate neighbours are. We shut the front door, have our tea and then watch TV and computer screens. We're 'atomized' – individuals with no real sense of 'belonging' to anything other than our own immediate families.

We also expect instant access to those things we desire. We define ourselves by what we own. Advertisements create a nagging sense of inadequacy in us that we attempt, unsuccessfully, to relieve by shopping. We've lost any sense of belonging to anything 'bigger' than ourselves. Only a few of us have firm religious beliefs. We no longer dream of a better, more progressive society. All this choice and freedom only makes us feel lonelier and more isolated.

THINK ABOUT IT We're uncertain nowadays about what we mean when we talk about a 'good person', and this is a problem, because being moral is mostly about **how to live with other people**. No one can sit in front of the TV being 'good' on their own.

The Greek philosophers thought that living with other people is what ultimately makes us truly human. Aristotle (384–322 BCE) said that anyone who lived without a community was either an 'angel' or a 'beast' – a saint or an incomplete human being.

So what have these ancient Greeks taught us? Think for yourself. Don't just accept the ideas and opinions of others.

Examine what they say and engage them in friendly argument. Socrates and Plato were both critical of their own society and government, and we should be too. So don't passively accept what politicians tell you. One obvious thing we can do is to try to help our own small community of individuals communicate with each other. The more people you talk to, the more you can evaluate and develop your own ideas. Being a good local citizen usually also makes you a happier person and, with luck, a wiser one too.

 Think for yourself. Try to find out before you judge.

---

2. Moral experts

The advisers

There are many people who are happy to tell you how to be 'a good person'. Sometimes they mean morally good, but usually they're talking about being a 'successful' person. Some of them are very helpful. Life coaches, gurus, therapists, counsellors, advisers, priests, philosophers, writers, psychic mediums, psychiatrists and your Uncle Harry will all let you know where you've gone wrong and tell you how to get back on track.

These experts on life may be worth listening to. There is a problem, though. We know there are experts on car mechanics who can fix cars. But are there really experts on life and how to live it?

Q Have you ever sought advice from an 'expert' in life's problems? Were they helpful? How were they helpful? What advice did they give you that was useful? Was it only useful for you, or could it be useful for everybody?

R There are experts in psychology, in relationship problems, in law, in employment, in life's problems. But there can't really be experts on morality. A priest or a counsellor can advise you, but in the end you are the only one who can make the decision.

Q Are some people better at making moral decisions than others? Why do you think they are? What do they have that the rest of us don't? (More experience of the world? More academic qualifications? A religious role in society? Other reasons?)

R When you're young, it's probably OK to ask for moral advice from adults who have had more experience of life. If you followed their advice, no one would blame you. When you're an adult, though, you can ask for advice, but only you can decide to ignore or follow it.

KEY FIGURE One philosopher who thought that some people were more knowledgeable than others was Plato (c. 428–347 BCE). He was the first truly systematic philosopher. He originally wanted to be a politician, but listening to Socrates changed all that. He eventually founded the Academy where he taught philosophy to young Athenians. His most famous work is *The Republic*, which begins with accounts of Socrates and his debates and ends with Plato's own description of a perfect society ruled by moral 'experts'. He also had some very strange ideas about what 'knowledge' is.

Like many Greek thinkers, Plato was in love with mathematics: geometric patterns and numbers. Mathematics is always the same and always true. 2+2 will always be 4. For ever and ever. It's eternally true, permanent, reliable and unchanging. And mathematics is somehow 'outside' of our world of continuous change and decay. So Plato thought that real knowledge had to be like this – immune from change and always true. Somewhere, along with mathematics, were all the ideal truths, he thought. The table I'm writing at is fine, but it won't last for ever, and so it's a second-rate copy of an 'ideal table' that's as true and permanent as numbers. Yes. I know it sounds odd. That's because it is.

Perfect rulers

Plato thought that this knowledge of 'perfect things' could only ever be accessed by a gifted few. They had a special kind of 'inner eye' that could 'see' numbers and the perfect templates of the 'copies' we see in our inferior material world. Holding all this system together was one big glowing idea – 'The Good'. Once you'd seen that, then you would be morally infallible. You'd always know what was the best thing to do, in all circumstances. This mental and spiritual gift would then promote you to the post of a ruler 'Guardian'.

Plato's ideal society or 'Republic' consists of three classes: 'Gold' people who are infallible and in charge, 'Silver' people who do the legal and bureaucratic administration, and 'Iron' folk who do all the work. So his ideal society would be like a beehive or ants' nest. Everybody knows what rank they are and what job they have to do.

The priest caste of Guardians tells everyone how to live and all ends happily.

So what's wrong with this story?

Well, lots. It's not clear why all knowledge has to be like mathematics. We know a great deal about things that change and decay. To say that biology or botany isn't real knowledge seems odd. But most of all, we can't accept that this kind of knowledge must be restricted to a gifted few. Why can't we read about it in the library, like all other kinds of knowledge? We can't believe that a few people would always be infallible. That's not how human knowledge works – it changes and gets thrown out or revised as we find out more. Our knowledge is fallible in a good way. We are also rather fond of the idea of democracy. One day we might want to get rid of these Guardians, so we'd like to be able to vote them out. No one likes the idea of permanent dictators, however wise and benign they are.

H.G. Wells, the famous writer of science fiction, had an interesting idea. He thought it would be better for everyone if we had a government of experts to run the country: people like scientists, economists, philosophers, architects, engineers and planners. After all, they know much more than ordinary people about what the country needs. They'd make the right decisions as opposed to popular ones. Think about global warming. A government of experts could make long-term plans for the planet's future. They wouldn't have to worry about being electable every five years. What we have now is government by amateurs who can only think short-term. It seems like a good idea to me. What do you think?

H.G. Wells' idea of 'government by experts' sounds sensible, at first. But think. We vote governments into power as **our** representatives. They may not know a lot about nuclear power, but they have access to experts who can tell them the facts and explain what the choices are. If they become unpopular we can vote them out. If we had H.G. Wells' panel of experts, they'd still get some things wrong but we wouldn't be able to vote to get rid of them.

Are there moral experts?

So do we believe in life experts? Do we think that morality is something we can leave to the gifted few? Some of us might prefer the idea of Plato's Republic, after all. If we were faced with a moral problem we could just 'phone a friend' and they would consult this special kind of knowledge and tell us the correct way to proceed. But living a life and being moral just isn't like that. We can't remain moral children who are told what to do.

Q Most people like to be told what to do – it's easier that way. Do you agree? Why? Why not?

R People who want to be told what to think and how to behave are probably confused, weak, or lazy. Someone once called them 'sheeple'. No one thinks that making your own moral decisions is easy. But equally no one can make them for you.

We have to try to do the right thing on our own. We can ask for advice, we can read books, but in the end, we have to make our own decisions and live with them. There are no moral experts. There are no gurus so wise and clever that they can lead our lives for us. Living successfully and being moral isn't a kind of **knowledge** at all. It's a matter of making **judgements** based on our own experience and our own principles. We have to choose what we think is the correct course of action and hope that we're more or less right. Being moral doesn't mean being obedient to a higher moral authority.

You are the only expert about your own moral opinions.

---

3. Religion and morality

The Good Book

Many people still believe that the best way to be a good person is to be part of an orthodox religious community. That way you're told what is right and what is wrong, and you have experienced religious leaders to advise you on more complicated moral problems. The three 'religions of the book' (Judaism, Islam and Christianity) present their followers with a list of rules and examples to follow. 'Being good' therefore means 'following God's word'. Moses brought ten eternal, universal and compulsory rules down from the mountain on two stone tablets. So morality is made simple. It is that which God has commanded. It's other-worldly, not something that human beings have invented.

Q Why do many religions stress that their commandments were discovered on mountain tops or in deserts, and not written by human beings?

R Prophets and gurus 'find' holy documents on mountain tops and hillsides. This reinforces the idea that morality emanates from a divine source and is not invented by mere human beings for their own benefit.

Q Should you always obey the voice of God? What are the problems with that?

R Are you sure it's God's voice that you heard? It might be wise to think about that. You could ask your friends what they think. Let's hope that God is asking you to do something that the rest of us also believe to be moral.

My friend Mary is a committed Christian, a member of a church whose congregation is shrinking year by year. Mary thinks that hardly anyone believes in God any more. She says there are lots of people who have no idea about what is right or wrong. Everyone these days is selfish and self-enclosed, talking into their mobile phones and ignoring those around them. All people are interested in is money and shopping. If we lose religion then we lose more than just going to church on Sundays. Do you agree with Mary or not?

Mary's assertions about the awfulness of modern life and the loss of faith are difficult to prove. How can you measure selfishness or greed? For most people, life has got better. Wages are higher, medical care is free (in many liberal democracies) and most people have a holiday once a year. We may be more selfish for lots of reasons: insecurity, the loss of community life, the need to compete in a capitalist society, the alienation of big city life. And lots of good atheists work for charities and help their neighbours as well as Christians. It's also easy to be nostalgic. Were people *really* better and nicer in the past? In Victorian Britain, church attendance was very high, but the poor were treated with ruthless contempt. There may be a connection between the decline in religious belief and the rise of individual selfishness. But if there is, it's probably not as simple as Mary thinks it is.

Socrates worried about this assumption that only religious people can be moral. He asked his friend Euthyphro what morality is, and Euthyphro sensibly said: 'That which is loved by the gods.' End of argument. But Socrates saw that there was a problem here. Are certain actions good, just because they are loved by the gods? Or do the gods love these actions only because they are good anyway? What if the gods loved wickedness and commanded you to kill or steal? Would that make killing and stealing good? Surely you would have to argue about that with the gods? Being blindly obedient to an arbitrary authority doesn't make you a good person, does it? Alternatively, what if the gods love certain actions only because they are inherently good anyway? If that's the case, then what difference does it make? If these actions are good in themselves, it presumably doesn't really matter what the gods say. So we don't actually need their approval to be moral. We already know what is right and what is wrong, independent of their commands.

Contradictions

There are other problems with religious doctrines. There are many examples in the Bible where God seems to contradict himself, and sometimes God's commands just seem odd – why is it wrong to eat shellfish, for example? Sometimes God seems to be ruthless and unjust to those tribes that aren't his chosen people.

And there are lots of atheists and agnostics around who are extremely moral, so religious belief isn't absolutely essential for someone to be a 'good person'. Socrates saw this straight away. For us it's harder. The Greek gods weren't especially moral, just powerful. So it was much easier for Greeks to see the difference between religion and morality. The Christian church has been around for a very long time, so many people, like Mary, still believe that morality can exist only in a religious context.

Q Most Christian theologians say that religious belief is not a matter of proof, but of faith. What does that mean, do you think, and do you agree? What does 'faith' mean?

R Faith is an odd idea. You have to take some things on trust alone. It means accepting the unlikely or the impossible without asking for proof. Some theologians think there's something wonderful about having to make 'a leap of faith' into religious belief. Philosophers, on the other hand, don't think you should accept anything without some kind of evidence or proof.

Religion and stability

Religions of all kinds generally want us to be good, usually focusing on that golden rule – **treat others as you would want to be treated yourself**. This golden rule seems to be a good starting point for someone who wants to be a good person. Jesus Christ said that you must do unto others as you would have them do unto you. The Chinese philosopher Confucius put the same point negatively: you must never do to others what you wouldn't wish them to do to you. The philosopher Immanuel Kant built a whole moral philosophy on this idea of 'universalizability' (moral rules have to be the same for everybody). Sometimes the golden rule doesn't work, though. Tastes differ. Just because I like chocolate doesn't mean I should insist that others eat it.

 The golden rule is about morality. It asks you to imagine what it's like to be other people. In other words, it emphasizes that the key component of all moral philosophy is *empathy* – the imaginative ability to place yourself in someone else's shoes. If you can't do this, or can't be bothered to do it, then you can't ever be a truly moral being.

Religious belief can also hold societies together and help to reinforce moral behaviour. Voltaire (1694–1778) said that, although he himself had serious doubts about God's existence, he was relieved that his servants were believers. He thought that if everyone, even servants, could decide for themselves what was right and wrong there would be moral chaos.

Q 'Religion makes me happier. It gives my life a sense of purpose.' Is that true for you? If it isn't, are you envious?

R If religious belief makes you happier, then good for you. But it's not for everyone. Some people might envy those who are convinced by their beliefs, but philosophers think that there's something very human, or even noble, about **doubt**. Doubting means owning up. We humans don't really know very much, but we'll keep on searching.

Being spiritual in modern life

Some people seem to need religion in their lives, probably because they have been brought up that way, and they like being part of a religious and cultural community. But even those who have no specific religious beliefs can feel a deep need for 'spirituality'. Religious traditions are dying out. Life is getting more complex. Most of us live in huge cities where we don't recognize anyone we know. We feel lost. And we still ask the old questions that used to have religious answers: 'There must be more to life than shopping, surely?' 'What is the purpose of my life?'

A more spiritual outlook can help people to survive mentally and emotionally in a society obsessed with materialistic goals. The philosopher Søren Kierkegaard (1813–55) said that a life devoted to consumerist pleasure is fine for a time but soon becomes addictive and then pointless and empty. Philosophical scepticism about orthodox religion doesn't stop us from searching for meaning outside of our daily existence. Most of us would agree that there has to be more to life than mere existence and the pursuit of material wealth.

FAQ

Can you be religious without being a member of a religious community?

You obviously can have spiritual feelings without being a member of an orthodox religious faith. We live in an extraordinary place – the universe – and you'd have to be very prosaic not to recognize that.

Meaning and purpose

Spirituality nowadays is not always bound to a traditional religious doctrine. It's quite possible to have experiences, intuitions and feelings that are 'spiritual' and to develop a 'religious' attitude to life without believing in an alternative reality or a supernatural being. Everyone has had feelings of awe and wonder when they look at the night sky and think about the vast expanse of the universe. Life remains full of mysteries.

Embracing a spiritual way of life can be beneficial. Psychiatrists report that spiritual beliefs give people a greater sense of meaning and purpose to their lives. Mystics of all religions have always said that meditation and prayer bring about a sense of the universe being interconnected in some way. It's obviously comforting to have a sense of belonging to something bigger than yourself. And there's no harm in thinking that our lives are a kind of journey towards increasing self-awareness and greater fulfilment.

IF YOU REMEMBER ONE THING

Religious beliefs are not the same as moral beliefs.

4. Human nature

Being good

So you want to be a good person? There are some philosophers who would say that you'll never get there. You can try as hard as you like, but you just can't make a silk purse from a sow's ear. You're human, after all, and made out of the same material as everybody else.

Everyone knows the plot of William Golding's novel, *Lord of the Flies*. Put some school kids on a desert island and it's not long before they're killing each other. And it's not really their fault. They're human beings and that's what human beings do to each other if there are no policemen to stop them.

KEY FIGURE This is also the view of the philosopher Thomas Hobbes (1588–1679). He was a royalist who supported the king during the English Civil War. He was horrified by the violence and cruelty of the war and the execution of Charles I. It made him very cynical about his fellow human beings. In his most famous book, *Leviathan* he tries to prove that the only way to restrain our selfish and ruthless desires is to subject ourselves to rule by an absolute monarchy. This kind of obedience was the only way we could ever escape from a life that would inevitably be 'solitary, poor, nasty, brutish and short'.

Q But if we are essentially bad, why do some individuals act so well? (Jumping into freezing water to save someone they don't know, for example?)

R Why do some people behave so well? Because there's no universal 'human nature'. Quite a few individuals are amazingly brave, generous and altruistic. Why? Well, we're all a mixture of various instincts and social conditioning. Most of us feel that we're duty bound to help anyone in danger, even if this sometimes also involves a degree of personal risk. And some of us are better swimmers too, and braver.

Being invisible

Socrates was more optimistic than Hobbes. He thought there was a better way of looking at human beings. He was trying to explain how to be a good person when one of his listeners, Glaucon, asked him a deceptively simple question. What would someone do if they possessed the magical ring of Gyges – the one that made you invisible? Glaucon said: 'No one would stick to what is right and keep his hands from taking other people's property.'

Glaucon is what philosophers call a **psychological egoist**. He thinks that all human beings are essentially wicked, but, again, it's not their fault. Blaming a human being for behaving badly would be like blaming a cat for killing a mouse. It's in their nature. We're all the same. If we behave well it's only because we fear being punished. If we were invisible and couldn't be punished, then we would soon start robbing banks or worse. After all, we're only human.

Q Over to you. You can make yourself invisible for as long as you like. Make a list of all the things you'd like to do. How many of them are illegal?

R So you were invisible. You shoplifted. You even robbed a bank. You chucked a pie into a politician's face. Or perhaps you only did good things like putting a £10 note into a beggar's hat. I'm not sure if Glaucon's test really tells you that much about human nature. Is it really true that we behave well only because we worry about being caught and punished?

Glaucon and Hobbes thought that we are all isolated individuals, only ever interested in our own selfish desires. I would disagree. We're social animals. We help neighbours and friends for many different reasons. We see it as an investment for the future (we may need help one day). We like others to have a good opinion of us. We rather enjoy being part of a community – it makes us feel more secure. So being good may itself be mildly selfish. Moral cynics may be right about a few wicked individuals who are genetically deprived or who had rotten childhoods. They may be right to think that in extreme and unusual circumstances, when a whole society breaks down, ordinary people's survival instincts can overrule fellow feeling. But thankfully such circumstances are rare, and societies thrive, not because we all walk around in fear of punishment by a strong government, but because of our belief in *reciprocity* and our need to *belong*. Most of us would soon get tired of that invisibility ring.

Human nature

What Socrates and Glaucon were arguing about is, of course, human nature. What are we 'really like'? There are lots of different views about this. You probably have your own. You think that most people, most of the time are, well, not too bad, even quite nice. Or you may think that most people are hypocrites. They pretend to be friendly, but basically they're selfish and greedy. They'll go for anything they think they can get away with. Your views about other people will usually determine your moral beliefs – how you should behave towards other people and they to you. This will probably influence your political views about how society should be organized. It will explain why there are social problems.

Q If there were no policemen or prisons, how do you think *most* people would behave?

R If there were no police or prisons, I suspect that most of us would carry on, trying to muddle through in a difficult situation. The real problem would be with those few individuals who behaved very badly indeed. It takes only a few empowered criminals to make life miserable and insecure for everyone else. This is always a major problem for anarchists, who believe that we can do without governments, police and prisons.

Q If you think we're all essentially good, why are there so many crimes in our society?

R There's no universal human nature, remember? So there will be criminals. Some benign moral philosophers will say that such people had bad 'moral luck'. They had awful childhoods, or they have addictive personalities, or they were somehow born greedy and ruthless. Nevertheless, didn't they choose to be like this as well? We all have bad impulses, but fortunately, most of us restrain them.

Good people and bad people

The view that there actually is something called 'human nature' is often criticized as 'essentialist'. If, like Glaucon and Hobbes, you believe that people are 'essentially' bad, then you will think that all talk about morality is pointless. What you will believe instead is the need for firm laws, a strong police force, and rigorous punishment for offenders. How else could society survive?

If you believe that human beings are 'essentially' good, then you will be in favour of a free and open society, even a kind of anarchism. Who needs governments if everyone can get on without them?

The problem is this: **is there such a thing as 'human nature' in the first place?**

Q Do you think we can generalize about all human beings like this, or is every single person different?

R I think we can generalize about people to a certain extent. We all need food, water, shelter and love, perhaps. Sociologists and psychologists think that there are many other things we all have in common. But it's probably wrong to say that all people are 'good', or all people are 'bad'.

From the start

Some philosophers, like John Locke (1632–1704), insisted that human beings are more or less blank sheets of paper when they are born, and then get written on by 'experience'. In other words, we're products of our social environment and our culture. The language we use, the way we classify everything, our relationships with others – all of it is 'cultural'.

THINK ABOUT IT

If you agree with this view, it means that when we think of something as being 'right' or 'wrong', it tells us more about our upbringing than anything else.

Nowadays we live in the age of genetics. Evolutionary psychologists say that we're products of our genetic inheritance. We're primates who possess all sorts of inborn drives and desires that determine how we think and feel. Human beings have adapted to an often hostile world and survived the ruthless competition of evolution. This means that our 'survival genes' may not be very attractive. Our ancestors had to be ruthless and violent, just to stay alive. Our closest animal relatives, chimpanzees, can be merciless and this can be used to reinforce this belief in a darker side to our primate nature. But then, meerkats are cuddly and cooperative, and this is also what we can be like, sometimes.

No one denies that we're animals. But we're very special, strange and unique animals, that's the problem.

What sort of question?

So it's a very complicated idea, this one of 'human nature'. It's very difficult for us to step outside of our own language, culture and prejudices in order to examine human nature objectively. Perhaps it will always be impossible to say exactly what 'human nature' is. Most of the human nature theories that do exist tend to be self-confirming and immune to debate. If you're pessimistic about human nature you'll say that all acts of charity are 'really' about self-promotion. If you're more optimistic you'll say that charitable acts are a sign of human goodness, and bad acts the result of a bad upbringing.

KEY FIGURE One man who thought that there was no such thing as 'human nature' was the French existentialist philosopher Jean-Paul Sartre (1905–80). He insisted that we are all free to choose who we are and what we become. Obviously we cannot escape a few biological drives, like those of hunger and sex, and we cannot remake our economic and social environment. A miner's son is going to be raised differently from a duke's. But the main truth about us is that we're all totally free to choose our own 'human nature'.

Most people don't like to face up to this. It's much easier to blame our genes or our parents or society for how we've turned out. But Sartre thought that this was wrong and cowardly. We have to admit that we're free. If we do, we will be truly human. We have to take responsibility for the person we've become. So there's a 'human nature' after all. Not one others have made but one we've constructed for ourselves. Unfortunately, we don't really know for sure how true Sartre's views are, or what his philosophy has to do with being a good person. If I freely choose to be a bad person, what would Sartre say?

Q What do you think? Do you agree with Sartre that we're the only ones to blame if we turn out to be wicked, or successful, or dull?

R Is Sartre right? Yes and no. We obviously have quite a big say in who we become. Our choices and actions do help to determine our character. But not totally. Our genes push us towards our futures, to some extent. Some people are born talented or more intelligent, and some just aren't. We have very little control over how we're raised. A happy childhood will usually make us feel more confident in life. Perhaps Sartre exaggerates his views to make clear a philosophical point about freedom and choice. And because he values freedom so highly, he has problems with someone who 'freely chooses' to be bad. But then, such a person would always be interfering with the freedom of others to choose, so a bad person can be condemned after all.

 IF YOU REMEMBER ONE THING You can't generalize about 'human nature'.

5. Choice and responsibility

Choosing

Aristotle was taught by Plato. He was a student for about twenty years, which probably annoyed his parents a bit. He was a good student, though, because he didn't swallow everything he was taught. He thought there was something wrong about Plato's 'moral experts' and Socrates' idea that a man who knows what goodness is will always choose it. He saw that this makes wickedness just a kind of ignorance.

Aristotle thought it was more complicated than that. If we want to be a good person, we have to be able to *choose*. And if we *are* free, then we're responsible for everything we do. If we choose to do something wrong, then we must be blamed and punished for it. But if you can't choose, then you're not guilty. So Aristotle was interested in 'imputability' – when you can be held responsible for choosing to do something bad.

Here are some cases for you to judge:

Q Ben is in a crowd at a football match when he's pushed from behind into another man who falls into the entrance tunnel and is killed. Is Ben responsible for the man's death or not?

R No. Ben at the football match was only an instrument, a thing. His body was pushed. He didn't choose at all.

Q 'I killed him. I admit it. He was having an affair with my next door neighbour. I just lost control. I'm sorry now that I killed my husband.' Is this woman morally responsible?

R She killed her husband in a jealous rage. She's guilty, but we might say that there were extenuating circumstances. The violence of her rage was so overpowering, it almost destroyed her freedom to choose.

Excuses and duress

Aristotle thinks that your actions have to be **voluntary**. You can't be held responsible for stealing a van if you were somehow compelled to steal it, or you were ignorant of the particular facts (perhaps you thought the owner had lent it to you). If you knew all the facts and your action was voluntary and deliberately chosen, then a criminal charge should be brought against you. If you were compelled to steal the van, then you have no responsibility at all for your action. (Two crooks kidnapped you and forced you to drive away.) This is because you haven't actually done anything – *something happened to you*.

But what about **duress**, a kind of mental and emotional compulsion? (The crooks told you they knew where you lived and one of them had a gun. He said he'd shoot your family if you refused to cooperate.) If the duress is severe, then you can't be held responsible. But if it's slight, then you might be. (The crooks said they'd steal your mobile phone if you disobeyed them.)

Q Kate is at home one day when two men burst into her house and take her kids hostage. They say: 'Either you bring home all your boss's takings for the day, or the kids get it!' Kate brings home the money, her kids are returned to her, the thieves run off. Is Kate morally culpable for what she did?

R No. The duress here is excessive. Kate has to protect her kids.

Q At a party, Jo is approached by a 'friend' who says: 'Take these drugs to John's house, or I'll tell everyone at this party that you're sleeping around.' She's horrified. She takes the drugs to John's but on the way there is arrested by the police for possession. Is she morally responsible for her actions?

R Jo is probably guilty. The threat to her reputation doesn't seem forceful enough to warrant committing a crime.

43

Inner compulsion

Nowadays we also recognize other kinds of compulsion that are 'internal', like kleptomania and certain phobias that are irresistible.

Q Gerry had a very unhappy childhood in which he was denied any presents on his birthdays. Consequently, he's now a kleptomaniac. One day he steals some car headlights from a shop, even though he doesn't have a car. Is Gerry morally responsible for his behaviour?

R Gerry seems to be in the grip of some mental illness. The stupidity of his theft (Headlights? He doesn't have a car!) points to this. So he's not really choosing 'freely'.

But what about drug addicts? Could we say that a craving for heroin was so strong that it led to the accused stealing a van? Or could we plead that, because the van owner had stolen the thief's wife, her husband took the van in a fit of passionate rage? (The law still distinguishes between unpremeditated acts and planned ones.) It's never easy.

Ignorance of the facts

What about ignorance? You can say 'I didn't know'. What didn't you know? That your brother's van had been sold to a new owner? This crime was, says Aristotle, unintended, and so not a crime at all.

 You see an advertisement in the paper for a cheap computer. You go round to see it at a stranger's house, like it and buy it. A week later the police come round and tell you it's stolen property and you may have to appear in court. Are you morally responsible for a crime? No. You bought the computer in good faith. You had no idea it was stolen. You were ignorant of the facts. So you're not guilty, as far as Aristotle is concerned.

But what about a man who shot his wife by mistake, not realizing that the gun was loaded? Nowadays we'd say that the gun owner was 'grossly negligent' for not checking the gun, and for pointing it at someone. He'd be found guilty of his stupidity and ignorance, but not of murder.

Ignorance of morality

What about the man who said, 'I didn't know what was going on'? Someone who was mentally ill and ignorant of who he was, what he was doing, to whom, with what, and how, probably is not imputable. To choose freely we have to know these things. But a man who said, 'I didn't know that stealing was wrong' would not be believed. He would be found guilty. In modern law this is still the case. **You can plead that you were ignorant of the facts of the case,**

45

but you can't plead that you didn't know what the law was.

Q Buster is a nice chap, but not very bright. Without mentioning it, he 'borrows' some money from his boss to pay the rent, and forgets to pay it back. At his trial he says: 'I didn't know that taking money and not paying it back was wrong.' Is Buster morally responsible?

R A lot depends on how stupid Buster is. It's hard to believe he didn't know that stealing is wrong. I'd give him a suspended sentence and a good telling off.

Q My dog chooses to pee on my carpet, even though he knows it's wrong. Is Fido morally responsible for doing this?

R Dogs can't be moral agents. They don't have the brains for it. Fido knew its owner was angry, but that's about it.

Are we really free?

This seems a rather odd question. (It's one that Aristotle was blissfully unaware of.) Of course we are, surely? I've just decided to come and type a bit of this book rather than go to the shops. I've made a cup of coffee rather than green tea.

CASE STUDY

If I decided to steal an iPod from a shop and got caught, I wouldn't plead not guilty on the grounds that I had no choice other than to take it. But what if I was **determined** by causes quite beyond my knowledge and control?

I don't think I'd get away with it, but perhaps I'd better explain. My argument to the judge would go like this:

- Every event involving physical things in the world has a cause.
- Human beings and their brains are physical things in the world, just like everything else is.
- Everything that they do must be caused, like all other events happening to physical things in the world. (Even if we don't yet quite understand the complex ways in which people are 'caused' to behave as they do. After all, people are very complicated.)
- Therefore human beings have no real free will.
- Therefore none of them can be held morally responsible for what they do.

Someone who believed all that would be called a 'determinist'. He'd say that everything physical is governed by the laws of nature, including me, so when I stole the iPod, it was inevitable. There's nothing I could have done to prevent it from happening. I am a physical organism made up of millions of cells, and they are made up of millions of

47

sub-atomic particles. My brain is the same. It fires off millions of electrical impulses all the time, making connections, and there's nothing I can do to control or alter any of that. So, when I stole the iPod, it was already inevitable.

The argument goes on, and on

I still don't think the magistrate would accept my defence. I'd be fined heavily and ordered to do some community service, probably. After all, it was my first offence.

And I'm positive it *was* me that chose to have coffee this morning. I can choose *now* to make a spelling mistak, even though the computer doesn't like it very much. I just feel free to do what I want, provided it's within my capabilities. I can't choose to float through the window or to speak fluent German, for example. But when I stole that iPod I knew it was the wrong thing to do. I've always wanted one, and it was so tempting. But it was *me*, not huge hidden forces, that chose to pinch it. When I say that I was 'free' when I stole the iPod, I mean that I acted voluntarily. I chose to steal. I wasn't forced to do so. This time my actions were caused by my choosing them. The opposite of 'free' is not 'caused' but 'compelled'.

Now you're a bit of an expert on free will and how to be a good person, have a look at these two puzzle cases:

Q Either you're going to be killed by a terrorist bomb or you aren't. It's all written down. So there's no point in taking precautions. What's wrong with this argument?

R Is there a book of fate? No. So precautions against terrorist bombs will limit the danger.

Q The government decides to put an end, once and for all, to these dreadful muggings. They round up all the young hooligans they can find and subject them to unpleasant aversion therapy. The result is that whenever they feel like mugging an old person, they feel violently sick. The result is no more mugging, safer streets and greater happiness all round. Do you think this kind of brainwashing would be justified? If it worries you, why does it?

R Brainwashing criminals may sound like a good idea. But we think that being human means being able to choose freely. In this case government is 'destroying' part of what it is to be fully human. Would it stop at criminals? It might be tempted to go a bit further. What about others who protested against it for perfectly valid reasons?

 There's more to being moral than knowledge. You have to choose.

6. Kant's maxims

Being a good person probably involves knowing a little bit about some of the most famous philosophical moral systems. You don't have to agree with them, but you might find them useful.

Kant: desires and duties

Immanuel Kant (1724–1804) thought that Christian ethics were about right, but he worried that they had no real philosophical foundation. To say that morality had been found on a mountain-top by Moses wasn't good enough. So he showed everyone how moral rules came from **reason**.

KEY FIGURE Kant was a very strange man. He lived a life of extreme regularity in the small German town of Königsberg, where he went for a walk at precisely the same time every single day. (Locals would set their clocks by him.) His servant, Lampe, always followed him, carrying an umbrella, just in case. Kant never married, although he seems to have enjoyed female company. He's one of the few people to have changed philosophy for ever. He finally sacked poor old Lampe for being drunk.

Kant began by stressing the need for 'goodwill'. You have to *want* to be good. And you have to be prepared to examine your motives carefully. So there would be little point in him talking to the Kray brothers. Kant also insisted that human beings have to be treated as 'ends' and not 'means', so you mustn't use people as if they were things. He maintained that being good is usually hard – doing your moral duty often goes against your inclinations. (I know I should babysit for my sister, but that would mean missing a really good party.) Kant was a rather austere and strict man. (I'd have to babysit.) But how am I supposed to know what the moral rules are? Where do they come from?

The categorical imperative

Kant said that we can find out what the moral rules are by using reason. And because reason is universal, the rules are also universal and consistent – the same for everyone, everywhere, in all circumstances. You can't water them down or make excuses.

So how do you work them out?

Kant's reasoning goes like this:

REMEMBER THIS!!!

You can act only on those rules [he calls them **maxims**] **that you are prepared to make into universal laws that apply to you and everyone else, all of the time.**

When you do that, you find that you end up with the usual prohibitions against lying, theft, murder and so on.

Not because God or Moses say so, but because **reason** does.

Kant explains it like this: what if you said, 'I think anyone should be able to tell lies if they want to'? If this were true, then everyone would start telling fibs, no one would know what 'truth' was, the meaning of language would implode and no one would be able to understand the difference between lying and truth any more. You've destroyed some key moral concepts and even the meaning of language itself. (If all you ever did was to tell lies, then you would really be talking a kind of nonsense.)

 This kind of 'universalizability test' ('What would happen if everyone …') is the bedrock of all moral rules.

And because they come from reason, these rules are compulsory or **categorical imperatives** and not optional.

Q If everyone stole, all the time, what would happen?

R If everyone stole all the time, the concepts of property and ownership would disappear. So stealing is irrational and therefore immoral.

The struggle

Kant's rules may be derived from reason but, he said, being moral will always be a struggle. If you act morally, you are usually going against your inclinations. You can't enjoy yourself. You have to do your moral duty, regardless of what you want personally. Kant makes this distinction clearer by contrasting two shopkeepers.

 One shopkeeper is **honest**, not because he's good, but because cheating customers is eventually bad for business. Word would get around. No one would shop at his place any more. He would go bankrupt. Better to be honest, then.

A **moral** shopkeeper is totally different. She doesn't cheat her customers because, well, it's just wrong. She'd be honest, even if she knew of a clever and secret way to cheat them. It's a bit of a struggle for her, though. (Think of all that extra money she could make, and no one would know!)

So perhaps you can tell a good person only by the fact that they look a bit miserable – they're always having to ignore their naughty desires. Morality is rational, objective, completely outside of our wants and desires. Kant's imperatives are a bit like Moses' commandments – non-negotiable.

Everyday life

Most of us break moral rules at some time or other, though. We lie about a friend's new dress. It doesn't make her look attractive, but we say that it does. We excuse a vagrant who steals from supermarket dustbins. We applaud someone who tries to assassinate a wicked dictator. And so on. Most of us think that moral rules are to be obeyed most of the time. They're useful generalizations. But sometimes moral rules can, or even should, be disregarded.

While many of us prefer to judge each case on its merits, some people prefer a set of clear moral rules. Kant's rules may seem inflexible, but at least you always know where you are. No one can plead that they're a special case. Kant thought that if you did break a rule, you would be diminished as a moral person. And when we examine human history we find many examples of 'bad' people doing absolutely horrible things to innocent people. If there were a few clear moral rules, we could condemn them or even persuade them to desist, perhaps.

Q You see a friend steal a wallet from someone's jacket. What do you do? You know that your friend is desperately hungry and has nowhere to live. The victim of the theft is very rich.

R Stealing is wrong. Full stop. Circumstances like the poverty of the criminal and the wealth of the victim don't count.

It's not an easy matter, ethics.

Problems

Most of us think that **motives** are important – we know the difference between accidentally scratching a car and doing it on purpose. But we also usually think that **consequences** are important too. We need to think carefully.

- What about a stalker, chasing our friend? Are we obliged to tell him the truth about where she is, or should we lie?
- And is morality always such a struggle? When we decide to do a good thing, like help an old lady across the road, it's not always a major fight against our inclinations. We walk away feeling a rosy glow of smugness.
- And what do we do if two moral rules conflict, as they sometimes do? It's the rigid inflexibility of Kant's moral system that is the main problem.

Q I gave my friend Harry a promise that I wouldn't tell anyone that he had given up his job and was just sitting in the park all day. Then I bump into his parents, who are worried about him. His mother asks me to tell her the truth about Harry. What do I do? How do I know which moral rule to obey? What would you do? Be loyal or tell the truth? Can you find a way of still being a good Kantian?

R This is a problem for Kantians. You have to obey two conflicting rules here: keeping your promise to Harry and telling the truth to his parents. You'd just have to say, 'I can't tell you. I made him a promise.' Or you could be evasive: 'I don't think Harry's very happy these days ...'

Q Your friend falls in love with a person you know to be really horrible. What do you do?

R You'd have to tell her the truth about her new boyfriend, but *only* if she asked you for your opinion.

Being consistent

Kant insisted that morality has nothing whatsoever to do with human wants and desires. It's something **objective**, not a useful generalization that we feel we can obey most of the time. Morality has to be consistent. There's no point in desisting from theft on Tuesday and going in for it on Wednesday because it's convenient.

So, provided we're always conscientious about everything we do, we can't go far wrong. Once we've worked out what the rules are, then, hey presto, all we have to do is obey them and we're moral beings and good persons. Kant said: 'Two things fill the mind with admiration and awe – the starry heavens above and the moral law within.' He really believed he had cracked the problem of finding what was the right thing to do. Myself, I'm not so sure.

 Try the universalizability test on these maxims:
- Cheat anyone who is foolish enough not to notice.
- Give away all your money to your neighbour.

Responses:
- If everyone cheated everyone else, then the concepts of honesty and cheating would disappear, just like the concepts of property and ownership. So it's not rational and not moral.
- If everybody exchanged their wealth with their neighbours, then some neighbours would benefit and others would lose. But the concept of ownership would go, so it looks as if it's an immoral idea.

Kant insisted that motive is the most important thing – consequences don't matter, not morally.

Q How would Kant judge a highly conscientious but incompetent car mechanic?

R Kant couldn't judge the incompetent but conscientious car mechanic on moral grounds. He might advise him to retrain, though. There does come a time when persistent incompetence becomes wicked. What if he reinstalled the braking system wrongly?

Q And what do we say to that stalker? 'Where's your friend living now?' he asks.

R As a Kantian, we'd have to tell the truth to the stalker. Or we could be clever and say, 'I don't know where she is', in the sense that no one knows **exactly** where someone is, at any one time (i.e. which room in the house she's in, and whereabouts in that room).

Q You buy a pair of trainers at a car boot sale. The guy behind the stall says: 'They're really cheap because my mate stole them.' What do you do?

R Stealing is wrong. Remember? Don't be an accessory to it by purchasing some hot trainers.

Obeying strict rules is one way of being a good person. If you think that moral rules are really important, and you think that everyone should try really hard to live by them, then Kant's moral philosophy may be for you. It might make you feel more secure that way, especially if most people agree with you that being a good person means 'following the rules'. But don't be fooled – it won't always be that simple or easy.

As a Kantian, you must stick to the rational rules.

7. Consequences

If you think that there's more to being a good person than just obeying a set of rules, then this moral system might appeal to you. It's less rigid than Kant's, but not without problems of its own. It says that motives aren't that important after all, only **consequences**.

Consequentialism or **Utilitarianism** is a very different kind of moral system from Kant's. It was made famous by Jeremy Bentham.

KEY FIGURE Jeremy Bentham (1748–1832) was an eccentric – he gave all his household utensils proper names, and he famously insisted that, after his death, his body should be mummified and propped up as an 'auto icon' for all to see. You can still see him in a glass case at University College London. He was a true democrat: he believed in one man, one vote, and in secret ballots. He was critical of most philosophy, calling it 'nonsense on stilts'. Unfortunately, he was also a rather grim authoritarian: he invented the dreadful 'Panopticon' – a house of correction where all of the prisoners could be watched, all of the time.

Utilitarianism: happiness sums

Bentham was a lawyer who saw that English law was a complicated mess. It needed to be based on one central basic principle if possible, and he thought he knew what that should be.

REMEMBER THIS!!! Bentham insisted that human beings are ruled by two 'sovereign masters': **pain** and **pleasure**. Any law that produced more pleasure and less pain for most people was a 'good' law, and one that produced more pain than pleasure was a 'bad' law. So the aim of all laws, and morality in general, was to produce good consequences – the greatest pleasure or happiness of the greatest number.

Utilitarianism is very democratic: it guarantees that the majority will always get what they want. If the majority of people want beer and cheap cigarettes, then that's what they get, provided these things produce happiness in the short and long term.

Bentham invented a system of 'happiness sums' (or 'Felicific Calculus') that showed you what to do as a good person. You try to work out what the consequences are for all your moral decisions. It works as follows.

CASE STUDY

Let's say you think it's about time your aged parents went into a home. Should you persuade them to go? You sit down with them and work it all out.

(1 means a small twinge of pleasure or pain; 20 extreme suffering or ecstatic joy.)

Pleasure

No more fear of an accident in the home.	+10
Luxury of having meals made, laundry done by others.	+8
No need to lug groceries back from the shops.	+4
No worries about maintaining house and garden.	+6
Company of others in the home.	+4
No more worries or inconvenience for children.	+8
Total	**+40**

Pain

Loss of independence.	−18
Loss of privacy.	−12
Boredom. Nothing to occupy the day.	−8
Having to sell and/or give away precious possessions.	−8
Total	**−46**

The sums show that there's more pain produced than pleasure, so the parents stay where they are.

Most happiness sums are a bit more complicated than that – you're supposed to measure pleasure and pain in terms of intensity, duration, certainty or uncertainty, how close or distant, how likely to produce other kinds of happiness, how pure – and very importantly, how many people are affected. Bentham was convinced that morality could now be made scientific, objective and measurable. His moral system was really designed for governments and local councils who had to pass laws and do 'pleasurable' things like building libraries and schools, digging drains and funding hospitals. Ratepayers had to feel that the 'pain' of paying higher taxes was justified.

 Here are some proposed laws for you to measure up. Get a bit of scrap paper and try to work out which ones should go on the statute book because they would produce more happiness than misery. (Some responses are given afterwards.)

- All cars to be low-powered and painted yellow.
- Examinations to be abolished.
- Soft drugs to be decriminalized.
- Anyone on state benefits made to wear a badge.

Responses:
- Yellow cars. People who would be happier are: road safety experts, people living in accident black spot

areas, environmentalists, and all those people who are no longer killed or maimed by speeding motorists. Car manufacturers would be miserable, as would their workers, owners of fast cars, the oil industry, and everyone who likes the idea of 'choice'. Working out the happiness sums would be very complicated indeed.

- A lot of students would be happier in the short term if there were no exams. But how could we be sure that they knew anything? Think of those airline pilots, dentists and doctors who were never tested. The long-term consequences don't look too good.

- If soft drugs were decriminalized then a lot of young people would be happy. But there would also be a lot of misery for those who will suffer health problems in the future, after years of drug abuse. Long-term misery might outvote short-term happiness.

- Who would benefit from this scheme? The shame of badge-wearing might drive a few proud individuals to seek work. It might discourage a few who were thinking of going on benefits. So taxpayers might be happier. But it would also lead to misery for those who actually deserve financial help. Bentham was quite ruthless: he was in favour of workhouses that stigmatized the poor but kept taxes down. He thought that capital punishment was a good thing – not because it punished one individual, but because it deterred others from acting wickedly. So the wearing of badges wouldn't have worried him that much. It worries us, though – why?

KEY FIGURE John Stuart Mill (1806–73) was a disciple of Bentham. He had been a child prodigy, force-fed with knowledge until he had a kind of nervous breakdown. He recovered through long walks in the country and eventually by the love of a good woman, Harriet Taylor.

Mill thought that Bentham's Utilitarianism and its methods could be used by private individuals like us, if we wanted to know what to do in our everyday lives. He worried a bit about 'pleasure', which sounded too physical and self-indulgent, and preferred the word 'happiness', which could include loftier activities like going to the opera and reading poetry. But you still had to do the sums.

Goodbye to the Ten Commandments

Utilitarianism is more radical than it looks. There's only one moral rule: always make sure that there's more happiness produced than misery, and then ensure that it's spread around. There are no other moral rules as such. Each individual decision or action is measured separately. You can lie, or steal, or even kill someone, if, by doing this, you produce more happiness than misery. And your motives don't matter. If you hack into a bank's computers to steal some money, get found out, agree to show the bank how you did it to escape prison and so help the bank to make its computers safer ... have you done a good or a bad thing, according to Bentham and Mill?

Here's another puzzle case for you to work out. (A response is also given.)

 A rich man makes a will, leaving all his money to his layabout son who everyone knows will spend the money on drink and gambling. So outraged is the rich man's solicitor, he secretly changes the will so that half of his client's money goes to Amnesty International. (He does this secretly so that he doesn't get caught, but mainly so that his behaviour isn't copied by other less moral solicitors.)

Think about all those political prisoners helped out with food parcels and legal advice. The dissolute son still gets a large amount of cash to waste on champagne and horses. The solicitor feels a glow of satisfaction. What traditional moral rules has the solicitor broken, and should he have done what he did? What would the Utilitarians say? What do you say? Do the sums from 1 to 20 and find out. Let's say the money helped 20 prisoners and got 7 out of jail.

Response:
It rather looks as if the solicitor did the right thing, as a Utilitarian. A lot of people are made happier. Provided he does this secretly, so that he doesn't set a bad example,

he gets away with it. But I'm not sure if I'd want him as *my* solicitor.

Hang on a minute

So what are the problems with Utilitarian ethics? It's certainly more flexible than Kant's rules – each case is judged on its merits, not by some inflexible law. Only consequences matter, not people's moral character, or even their motives. People get what they want. Morality also depends on circumstances – who, what, where you are. A mother would probably be allowed to steal a loaf of bread from a rich baker, to feed her starving child.

Nevertheless, this kind of moral flexibility is a bit worrying. Quite a lot of people would feel happier if everyone just obeyed the rules. We know what they are. Everyone knows where they stand. No one would be making secret calculations behind our backs to see if it was OK to steal our new car, or lie to us about how much something cost.

There are other problems with Utilitarianism, some more serious than others. You have to decide on these for yourself:

- Are human beings merely primitive organisms that respond only to pleasure and pain?
- Can you really *measure* happiness?
- Would any of us actually have the time to do these sums?

- Is it really possible to calculate all the consequences of our decisions?
- How can we ever really know what will happen in the future?
- What if the majority of people voted for things that experts know may give them short-term pleasure but long-term misery, like cheap cigarettes?
- Do we give people what they want or what governments think is good for them?
- Can the majority never be overruled?
- And what about traditional moral rules? Can we really do without them?

Mill's solutions

Mill tried to answer some of these criticisms. He thought that ordinary people like us could stick to the usual moral rules most of the time, even though that wouldn't make us very Utilitarian. Only occasionally, when a difficult moral problem presented itself, would we have to sit down and work out the consequences. We would also have to make educated guesses about the future.

THINK ABOUT IT Mill was worried about 'the tyranny of the majority'. For example, most people are suspicious of gypsies and might be happier if this small minority was locked up. So what happens to the rights of minorities in these cases? Mill was a **pluralist** – he believed that a variety of views and life-styles was a good thing. That way, societies change and progress. Everyone should be allowed to live their lives more or less as they want, including gypsies, provided they don't interfere with the happiness of others. Laws, like those against homosexuality, should be repealed if no one is harmed by what they legislate against.

But Mill was also a culture snob. What if most people wanted endless repeats of TV soap operas and *Big Brother* shows? Perhaps 'educated' people should be allowed more 'happiness votes' so that opera, modern art and difficult novels would survive. So, when push came to shove, Mill also thought that there probably was more to morality than just majority rule. He also worried about motive. Surely it was still important? Although consequences were the main consideration, he thought that people should act 'conscientiously' as well, which isn't very Utilitarian of him.

Q A doctor is looking after a cancer patient who is very depressed. The doctor decides to lie to his patient and tell him he is recovering, even though he isn't. The lie will make the patient much happier. It won't affect the doctor much. (But do think of the long-term effects this might have. What about the man's relatives, people's trust in doctors, those who are told truthfully by their doctors that they are getting better, the doctor's moral character?) Is the doctor justified in telling this small lie, as a Utilitarian? If not, why not?

R The doctor who lies to his patient is acting out of kindness. His white lie seems to be justifiable. But think of all of the bad consequences. In the long term we like to think that doctors will tell us the truth. It's not as easy as it looks. It might be better to trust to the doctor's own judgement. But that's another kind of moral philosophy.

Q By torturing a terrorist we can save the lives of many innocent civilians. So, should we, as good Utilitarians, torture him? If the answer to this question is yes, does this worry you? If so, why?

R Torture is so vile that it's difficult to see how it could ever be justified. The short-term consequences look good. We find out where the bomb is. But what if governments are encouraged to think that acts like waterboarding are acceptable? This is where it might be better to be a Kantian for once.

Q When Scott of the Antarctic was returning to base, one of his men became injured. He asked Scott to abandon him and save all the others. Scott refused to do this. Because carrying a stretcher slowed all the party down by two days, they weren't rescued and they all died. Was Scott a good Utilitarian or not?

R If he was a Utilitarian, Scott probably made the wrong decision. It's just a matter of numbers. One dies but four live. However, let's not be too hard on him. Scott couldn't see into the future. It's easy for us to condemn him, but he did act out of loyal comradeship.

Q By chance, a brain surgeon and a tramp find themselves on a waterlogged raft, having been shipwrecked. The raft is about to sink. It won't hold two people. The brain surgeon pushes his companion overboard, and keeps the murder a secret from everyone when he's rescued (so that he doesn't broadcast his behaviour and encourage it in other less valuable people who may get shipwrecked themselves one day). He saves thousands of lives later on in his career. Is he a good Utilitarian? Is he a good man? Is there a difference?

R The brain surgeon murdered the tramp. This is one of those puzzle cases loved by philosophers who want to test a moral theory to destruction. Utilitarians would have to approve of the brain surgeon's act, but that doesn't seem to mean that he's a good man. See how difficult morality can be?

Utilitarianism is what informs most government decisions today. Civil servants talk about 'cost benefit analysis' when they advise ministers. Governments in a liberal democracy don't really think it's their job to make people happy – that's up to each individual. But they are in the job of reducing suffering – which is why they fund the National Health Service in the UK, for example. Nowadays, modern Utilitarians tend to talk about people's 'interests' rather than their 'happiness', partly because happiness is a very relative and personal thing. It's certainly possible to adopt and adapt Utilitarianism as a personal moral philosophy, though, as we've seen, it has unique problems of its own. But that doesn't mean that we shouldn't think about our actions and try to predict how much happiness they will cause. That too is part of being a good person.

IF YOU REMEMBER ONE THING

For a Utilitarian, it's the greatest happiness of the greatest number that counts.

8. Good people

So. We've got a moral problem. What should we do? Do we look at all of the moral rules that are produced by Kant's method and obey the relevant one, even though we don't particularly want to? Perhaps. Or do we sit down and work out what would produce the greatest happiness of the greatest number, and do that? Maybe. Should I tell a lie? 'No', says Kant. End of story. 'Well', say the Utilitarians, 'it depends on the consequences.' Is that all there is to being a good person? Sometimes these moral systems seem remote and theoretical, abstractions from life rather than a part of it.

THINK ABOUT IT

Most of us know how to behave, more or less, most of the time. How? Because we've been well brought up by our parents, and then influenced by a few teachers and some good friends. If we're over 30, we've also had some experience of the world and now have a good idea about what it means to be 'moral'. We know when to be sympathetic and helpful and when to show someone the door. We've been brought up to be good and now we've had a bit of practice at it. Our mother told us to let that tedious kid from next door play with our model railway, so we did. Later on we were reprimanded for stealing plums off next door's tree.

And this is what morality is usually about – being a good person intuitively, as opposed to obeying rigid rules or making lengthy calculations. It's become a habit.

So perhaps it's time we looked at moral *people* and not moral *systems*.

Aristotle again

This is what Aristotle did, a long time ago. He said that we're all born with innate tendencies, some good, some bad. What we need to do is nurture and encourage the good tendencies and repress the bad ones, especially in children and adolescents. If you do this, then, with a bit of luck, you'll produce adults who are honest, kind, and brave. They will be citizens who behave well towards others in their community. After a while it's in their nature to be good.

Aristotle's very different sort of moral philosophy is called **virtue ethics**. (But take note: 'virtue' has changed its meaning. It now has associations of a rather stiff Victorian kind. All Aristotle means by it is something like 'character traits' or 'types of behaviour'.)

Virtue ethics is a different approach to ethics – a mixture of philosophy and psychology. It asks what sort of people we should be.

Aristotle believed that you couldn't be scientific about morality. Everyone's different, situations are unique. How can you possibly subject everything to one moral rule? He thought that people have to rely on their 'practical' wisdom, not on some abstract theory. It's the sort of wisdom that's everyday, rough and ready. Theoretical wisdom is what you need to be a mathematician or philosopher. Practical wisdom is the wisdom of the carpenter who knows, more or less, what wood to use, and how to build a roof. It's a matter of experience and know-how. Morality is inevitably always a rule of thumb affair – something you can only get roughly right. No one is ever going to be perfect at it.

Flourishing

Aristotle thought that we all had to use this practical wisdom so that eventually we reach a state of 'eudaimonia'.

Eudaimonia meant something like 'happiness' or 'flourishing' for the ancient Greeks. We don't really have an equivalent word because it's a concept that emerged from a specific culture, very different to ours. Athenians thought that everything had an ultimate purpose or function that made it 'good'. A good knife was sharp, a sheepdog a good herder and so on. Human beings were different from knives and dogs, but they still had an ultimate function. We are different because we are **rational**. So good humans (i.e. good examples of our species) use their reason to its fullest

extent. Reason is a virtue in itself, admirable for what it is –
not just a useful tool.

A young Athenian would be encouraged to cultivate
a whole package of 'citizen virtues' like tolerance, sympathy, courage, conviviality, and so on. Learning to be sympathetic is good for your character and it makes you feel
good. Eventually sympathy becomes almost instinctive, a
pleasurable disposition rather than a struggle. We cultivate
certain virtues inside ourselves like sympathy and tolerance, and then become 'successful' human beings, happy
and 'flourishing', living in a healthy society that's cohesive
and strong.

So now 'a good person' has two meanings – being morally
good, and being a good example of humanity. For Aristotle
they are the same thing. For us too, most of the time.

The middle way

So what *should* we do if we want to grow up as successful
human beings? One essential thing is to control our emotions. Thoughtless and extreme feelings of anger, jealousy
and fear often lead us into trouble. We can't flourish if we're
always getting drunk and fighting, or spending our free
time envying the neighbours. What we have to do is be
as rational as we can, when we face all the worrisome situations of everyday life. If we can do that, we will become
more mature, less childish.

It's not always easy to overcome feelings of indignation or greed – we're human after all. But if we try to overcome 'bad' feelings like jealousy and rage, then we will make progress. Emotional discipline will become easier, more automatic. We will be more tranquil and the struggle will become less demanding. This means that when we're faced with a moral dilemma we won't panic, get furious or make rash judgements. It's a matter of finding the right **balance** between indignation and indifference.

If we see a friend of ours stealing an innocent stranger's wallet, we don't get violently angry, but we don't walk away either. We choose the 'mean' between the two. We give our friend a severe talking to and insist that they return the money. However, if we see a man repeatedly hitting a small child, then we should get very angry indeed and wade in there and stop him.

It all depends – on the situation, the people involved, our relationship to them, and the nature of their behaviour.

Being consistent

There are no hard and fast moral rules. Each moral situation we find ourselves in demands a specific judgement, and sometimes action, from us. It sounds difficult, but as we get older and wiser, it gets easier. We keep on being moderately generous to those who deserve it, and maybe even to those who don't, on occasion. If we're like this most of the time, then having charitable feelings about the less fortunate will become virtually automatic, because we've become, well, a nice person.

 If we already have the disposition to be sympathetic to others, then we will act correctly in those situations where sympathy is appropriate. Such dispositions need to be well established and fixed so that they are **reliable**. We can't be moral if we keep changing our minds.

Being consistent might sometimes be hard work. We will be faced with drama queens or idiots mired in troubles resulting from their own recklessness and stupidity. But we must grin and bear it. We know how to choose the appropriate 'mean' by now. We don't have to be wholly indulgent. We can be supportive but also show them how to avoid future disasters, and how to stand on their own two feet.

Social beings and moral relativism

Aristotle lived in a crowded city state, so he knew that humans are social animals who have to get on with each other. For him there was no real distinction between ethics and politics. He believed that we have to take our social duties seriously. We flourish best only when we are good neighbours and citizens. We're not hermits. We must be tolerant, generous, sociable, thoughtful and kind – and we expect the same from others. It's **people** we have to think about, not actions or rules.

Aristotle's ethics seems like old-fashioned common sense much of the time. It all sounds sensible, but it isn't exactly crystal-clear. We're not ancient Greeks, so how do we know what the blueprint for a good human being is? Do we really know the purpose or function of a human being? Do human beings have one single purpose? Who decides what qualities we need to become good examples of humanity? Perhaps all we can do is rely on educated guess-work. We know that we are social beings and so need social skills. But is that all?

Virtue ethics can be criticized for being little more than traditional codes of practice – those enshrined beliefs that individuals need if they are to fit into a specific kind of society. But societies are different, so what counts as a good person will be different.

THINK ABOUT IT It's unlikely that the moral virtues of a medieval Chinese monk would be of much use to a modern citizen of New York. Ancient Athenian women were expected to possess the female virtue of servility and to be quiet and placid. Female 'virtues' like these have a clear ideological purpose. They favour the group in power – men – more than others

– women and children. But is this a problem? It all depends on what you expect from a moral principle.

If you think that morality should be universal, true for all societies and all times, then it doesn't look as if virtue theory is for you. Some virtue theorists respond by insisting that it's only those virtues that *are* universal that count as virtues. But virtues remain inevitably relative – they evolve out of specific societies and are relevant only to that society.

How do I know what to do?

Virtue ethics isn't always very helpful for someone who wants to know which **actions** are moral and which aren't. Someone who stole a wallet would be accused of lacking the moral virtue of trustworthiness, which is a rather odd kind of condemnation. We might prefer to say they had committed a wicked act. Virtue ethics doesn't produce an acceptable code of moral conduct or a set of rules. There may be ways out of this dilemma. We could vote for a few individuals we believed to be extremely virtuous and ask them to produce a set of universal moral rules that we all had to obey. But that wouldn't be virtue ethics.

Problem cases

In spite of all these problems, virtue ethics can often seem sensible and human. It admits that ethical judgements can never be calculable and precise – people and situations will never be quite the same every time. Applying a system of rigid rules to everyday experiences may not always work. Rules conflict or may not be appropriate because they don't take into account your relationship with another person, or the uniqueness of the problem you are both trying to solve.

Here are some situations to think about. What's your rule-of-thumb moral judgement?

Q Should I tell my friend the truth about her cheating boyfriend?

R See how difficult it is? Should you tell on the cheating boyfriend? What if the news is devastating for your friend? What if you heard about the immoral boyfriend from the often unreliable gossip grapevine? How long-standing is your friendship? Are you wise and experienced enough to decide?

Q Should I join an illegal protest against global warming?

R How important is global warming? Is it best to obey the law, or help to save the planet? What if your illegal protest puts the lives of some people in danger? Are you acting moderately in the circumstances, because the danger to the planet is so severe? Or are you being an extremist?

Q Should I provide a false alibi for my thieving brother?

R You know your brother is desperate and only stole food to feed his starving family. So do you back him up or tell the truth in court? What does your wisdom and experience of life tell you to do? Is your brother a special case? Why is he?

Although it's been around for a long time, there's still a lot of hard thinking to be done if virtue theory is to become as influential as Utilitarianism and Kantian ethics. It's not always clear where and how moral psychology is relevant to moral philosophy. What virtues are appropriate for our own times? Are they the same ones that Aristotle recommended? Are there others, like creativity, the ability to adapt to change or environmental awareness? Is being fiercely competitive and successful a virtue or not? It's not easy.

More problems

Now you know all about virtue theory, here are two people for you to think about. Are they good or bad, according to virtue ethics? What would Kant say about them with his objective rules? Have they increased or diminished the greatest happiness of the greatest number? Is there anything else that worries you about them?

CASE STUDY

Susan: *My uncle has just defrauded a widow of a small amount of her savings. But he's a lovely old chap, a bit of a rogue, and the widow has no idea, apparently. She seems to have fallen for him too. It would break her heart if she found out. I told him never to do it again. I don't know of any rule about defrauding willing victims. That's the trouble with all of this moral philosophy – there are no simple answers.*

Susan thinks that virtue theory is so relative that life is a kind of moral free-for-all. Each moral decision depends on the individuals involved – the judge and the judged. But at least we know where we are with Kant. He'd say her uncle was wicked. Full stop. He broke the objective, universal rules (against stealing and lying). Utilitarians would also condemn her uncle for setting a bad precedent. Stealing nearly always produces more misery than happiness, so her uncle would have to be a very special case if he were to be excused. Maybe Susan doesn't have the experience or wisdom needed to make a mature moral judgment. It's true that virtue ethics isn't always helpful when it comes to evaluating tricky moral situations like this one. Perhaps Susan should ask what a more experienced person would do in this situation. Or she could rely on a panel of mature advisers to help her and just do what they recommended. Or perhaps sometimes there just aren't simple solutions for every moral problem.

CASE STUDY

Mike: I'm a rat. I always was a rat. My father was a rat. My whole family were rats. I was taught how to nick stuff as soon as I was a nipper. My mates were all rats as well. I didn't meet those that weren't. Let's face it. I was badly brought up. My 'virtues' are dishonesty, lying, violence when required, and a contempt for those that aren't rats. Maybe I was unlucky in how I was brought up. But that's not my fault, is it? You can't blame me for what I do for a living.

Morality is partly about being blamed or praised for what we do. But what if we're born to bad parents, grow up in morally bad surroundings, make unsuitable friends, follow inappropriate role models, and see society as unfairly punitive? Our 'virtues' will then not be those that make good citizens. And that may not necessarily be all our own fault. The law certainly expects people to take responsibility for their actions, though. A plea of 'I was badly raised' wouldn't get you off in court. It's hard for us to believe that Mike didn't know he was doing bad things. He's not a psychopath, just bad. Kant did stress the need for good moral education, but he still had little time for weak-willed individuals. The Utilitarians would condemn Mike for the misery that he produced. His character wouldn't enter into the happiness sums at all. But virtue ethics would say that Mike experienced 'bad moral luck' because of the way he was brought up. Some people may be better at shaping their character than others. His moral character may not be wholly his own fault. All we could do is try to intervene. Educate him into thinking differently, if possible. But 'bad luck' like this is a problem, especially if moral **character** is our main concern.

Life is complicated, that's the trouble. Moral rules can offer guidance and a way of analysing any given situation, but obeying them at all times may not guarantee that you will do the right thing, however conscientious you are. Being a good person seems to be partly a matter of **experience**, **perception** and **maturity**. We need to know the nature of the characters we're judging, their histories, their present situations and how wicked their actions actually are. Moral judgements have to be **flexible** and **adaptable** and **relevant**.

Are we virtuous today?

Nowadays we think about ourselves and our relationship to society in a very different way. But this doesn't mean that virtue ethics has to be historically remote and irrelevant. Most modern parents recognize that children are born with a whole set of character traits – rage, selfishness, jealousy and intolerance, as well as sympathy, love, patience, and determination. They try to encourage the good ones and stamp on the bad ones so that their offspring become more civilized and easier to live with. This kind of moral education continues throughout adolescence and beyond – we are raised into virtuous behaviour by parents, teachers, friends, priests, role models and colleagues at work.

 Virtue ethics is also still a useful method of questioning and criticizing the belief that morality has to mean obedience to a set of inflexible rules. It places much more stress on human psychology, emotions and relationships with others. We grow up in families, schools and colleges, the workplace, communities, and society as a whole. We practise social virtues all the time so that we eventually come to recognize what good and appropriate behaviour looks like. We grow up. We become mature adults. We are sympathetic because we know that this is the right way to behave and it makes us feel fulfilled and happy. We feel that we belong. That's the idea. We aren't isolated individuals fighting everyone else on behalf of our families. We are part of a 'Big Society'.

That's enough moral theory for a bit. Now you know the three important moral theories. There aren't any others, unless you want to return to a morality sanctioned by religion, or you've decided to become a nihilist with no morals at all. The important thing is to do what Socrates said: think. Make your own mind up. Don't be swayed by the opinions of others, unless you think they've made a very good case. But do listen to other opinions, especially those of your friends. And here they are. The next subject for discussion.

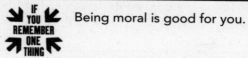

IF YOU REMEMBER ONE THING Being moral is good for you.

9. Friendship

Epicureans

Most people would say that someone without any friends is sad, lonely and not a very 'good person' – meaning that they aren't fully 'human' in Aristotle's sense. They wouldn't achieve their full potential. They wouldn't flourish.

KEY FIGURE The philosopher Epicurus (341–270 BC) wrote about friendship. By this time, Athens had declined, and there was little point in discussing what it meant to be a committed citizen in a democratic city state. Athens had become an insignificant town in a hugely powerful empire. Only the private individual remained. So the good life had nothing to do with being a citizen.

The Epicureans withdrew from public life altogether and spent their days with like-minded friends, pursuing a life of happiness in their own houses and gardens. The 'garden philosophers' engaged in endless discussions about religion, death, pleasure and friendship. They agreed with Aristotle that a happy individual is one who is moderate in all things – enjoying both mental and physical pleasures, but not dominated by them. They valued friendships of all kinds. They thought that being a friend is good for you: it makes you a happier person, but also a better one. It helps

91

you to become more tolerant and sympathetic than you might otherwise be. The good life was now about talking to your friends, surrounded by flowers and trees.

Philosophers like Epicurus had to think about personal survival in a world where the individual counted for little and had no political say. In some ways it was a bit like how our lives are now – coping with a world of large impersonal governments and mysterious and powerful corporations. All we little people can do is work out how to live our lives as best we can.

Friendship and love

So what is friendship? The Greeks, as always, had a word for it.

It's not **agape** – the love that God has for us and that we are supposed to have for all humanity. It's not **eros** either – I don't have sexual relationships with my friends. The word we need is **philia**, which means something like affection.

Love and friendship aren't quite the same. Friendship is psychological, not physical. And love, alas, is all too often unrequited, whereas friendship isn't – it can't really exist if it's not reciprocated. Friendship has to be mutual, and it implies a degree of unselfish concern for someone else. Friendship helps us to develop a sense of empathy – using our imagination to put ourselves in our friends' shoes. It enables us to relate to people with lifestyles and views different to our own.

But friendship isn't just a training ground. Friendship also gives us pleasure and enjoyment as well as benefiting us in other ways (especially if our friend is a plumber). However, if a friendship exists only because it benefits us personally, then perhaps it's a lesser kind of relationship. Kant would say that friends have to be *ends in themselves*, not means. Friendship has 'intrinsic', not mere 'instrumental' worth.

THINK ABOUT IT Most of my friends are caring parents. Some of them believe that they can be friends with their children. But the parent–child relationship is unequal – the parent can tell a child to eat cabbage and go to bed at 8.00pm. A child can't reciprocate, so the relationship is unequal, and so it can't really be called a friendship. Friends are usually 'equal' in the sense that one isn't greater or lesser than the other.

What is friendship?

Friendship involves mutual caring. Philosophers would call it a **necessary condition** for friendship to exist at all. No caring, no friendship. You're sympathetic to your friends, you're committed to them, you're prepared to help them, you enjoy their successes and regret their failures. You want them to be happy. They're valuable because of the specific qualities they possess. You laugh at their jokes, you're more or less as intelligent as they are, you share a kind of 'dialect' built up over time.

Q Do people consciously choose their friends, or do friendships just happen?

R Friendships just seem to happen. There are some people you find it easy to get along with, and some that you don't. 'Choosing' a friend seems a bit calculating, perhaps.

Sometimes friends change – they get married, for instance, and you have to cope with their new values and interests. If the change is drastic, then the friendship may shift from 'close' to 'casual'. So the relations of friendship are unlike those of family. I can let friendship lapse but I can't stop being a son or brother.

Friendship also requires work. You need to be patient and flexible. Friends can bore you rigid with their new enthusiasms and fads. Sometimes you can mock them gently, at other times you have to simulate an interest. It's a good idea to be conciliatory if you offend them in some way and be prepared to accept criticism yourself. You have to be tolerant when they're being impossible. You have to spend time with them and communicate your own ideas and views as well.

USEFUL TIP

Friendships are between equals. So don't be a doormat. It's a good idea to be assertive but not aggressive and to avoid too much personal abuse. Friends can be very demanding but are also very good value – you learn how to be patient, flexible, empathetic, diplomatic, and open to new ideas.

Close friendships, trust and sharing

So what is close friendship? One obvious feature is that you're prepared to confide in a close friend. You tell them stuff you wouldn't tell anyone else. So friendship involves trust. You trust in your friends' feelings of goodwill towards you. You wouldn't make yourself vulnerable to someone who was merely an acquaintance. You also tend to trust your friend's judgement – they know how to keep quiet, and when to advise.

Q What if your friend told your secrets to someone else? Could you ever be friends with them again?

R Friendships rely on trust, so it would be hard to forgive a friend who didn't keep a secret. But then if the secret was rather trivial and your tolerance levels high, then you could forgive them. But I wouldn't tell them a secret again if I were you.

There's also more to friendship than keeping secrets.

- You share ideas, values, attitudes, beliefs.
- You agree about what is important and valuable in life.
- You agree on what is good, pleasant and attractive.
- You share ways of thinking.

Aristotle thought that close friends would usually agree on the best ways to live a life, and about what counted as fulfilment and happiness. This is often why friendship leads to shared activities. Friends just enjoy each other's company. They share experiences and talk about them. These interactions may often be quite frivolous and unproductive. It's the sharing that counts. And not just secrets but also ideas, actions, emotions, pleasures and achievements. So, provided you take your friends' views, beliefs and values seriously, you aren't obliged to share them all. The same goes for your friend. Nevertheless, no one would deny that sharing makes friendship less like work or some kind of duty. As always, Aristotle thought it was usually a question of balance and moderation.

So you and your friends tend to agree about politics, current events, art, music, sport and so on, *most of the time*. But sometimes it's possible to have a friend whose ideas and values are radically different to yours. It's also quite possible to share many values and beliefs with people who are not, and never could be, your friends.

Mutual influence

It's often been said that married people tend to end up looking like each other. Similarly, friends can influence each other's ideas, tastes and beliefs. They become 'another self', according to Aristotle. Complete agreement about everything may not always be a good thing, though. We obviously like it when our prejudices and grumbles are reinforced, but we should also be forced to re-examine them. If your friend challenges your habit of smoking cannabis, you're forced to re-evaluate your tastes and examine your ideas and beliefs, and so you come to know yourself rather better. So friendship may function a bit like therapy in this respect.

Most friendships will be good for you, but not all. Your friend may be a keen gardener, or she may be an enthusiastic gambler. Perhaps we should say that a true friend always has your long-term interests at heart. I'd stick with the gardener.

REMEMBER THIS!!! You have to invest some care for yourself and your own values. You want to remain an autonomous individual. You don't want to be swamped by the ideas of somebody else, however dear to you they are. It's an alliance, not a complete takeover.

Flourishing

Friendship can also change you for the better. Your friend insists that you go to the opera, and wants you to share her love for country dancing and detective fiction. You find that you really enjoy opera and detective fiction and so become a more interested and interesting person. You flourish more thanks to your friendship.

Sometimes a friend can even have a moral role, when they force you to re-evaluate your beliefs and prejudices. We believe that our friends will tell us the truth most of the time, so we listen to what they say.

THINK ABOUT IT

Friends can also be a useful sounding board – we can test out our new ideas, relationships, activities and plans on them. However, be warned. Most of us are prepared to go along with our friends' harmless self-deceptions. Everyone likes to think that they're more attractive, intelligent, funny and wise than they probably are. No one would want a friend who was rigorously truthful at all times. This raises the question of honesty. Could we put up with a friend who was always brutally honest?

Perhaps we all need some delusions to remain cheerful. We don't expect our friends to be our moral guardians. We might be more ready to accept criticism from disinterested parties like a psychological counsellor or a life coach. It's not easy. It would depend, most of us would say. And *country dancing* – are you serious?

Friendship and communities

So why is friendship so important to us, as human beings? Why are we happy to devote time and resources to it? Aristotle would say that having friends is part of our nature. We can't flourish without them. Friends enhance our lives as individuals. But, like families, they also help to make us part of a community. Families join together to do something about the graffiti on the walls outside the local school. Friends volunteer to distribute party leaflets at election time, or help to maintain a local football ground. They talk endlessly about each other and their social life on Facebook. If we have friends we can feel that we are part of a community, not isolated from the world.

Friendships also benefit society as a whole. A Utilitarian would see how friends care for each other. This increases the well-being of all, in small amounts. And if the habit of friendship leads to greater cohesion in community life, then that's even more 'happiness' being created and spread around.

Q Millionaires tend to congregate in gangs because they feel less awkward that way. Could a millionaire and a bricklayer ever be true friends? If not, why not?

R The millionaire and the bricklayer *could* be friends, but it would always be a rather awkward relationship. Friendships, alas, tend to be between people who are more or less equal, and that obviously includes levels of affluence.

Is friendship moral?

Friendships usually have a history. This means that friends share a sense of 'belonging' – partly because they have adapted to each other's thought processes and habits over time. This makes them unique to us. Because of this shared past they cannot be 'exchanged' for similar individuals. If a friend suffers from depression or becomes an alcoholic, we don't think about swapping them for someone else.

Strangely, this poses a major problem for moral theories. For Aristotle, friendship is moral because it enables individuals and communities to help each other to flourish. So we can be a good person and a friend. The two are mutually supportive. There's no problem here. But Kantians and Utilitarians tend to focus on **impartial** and **objective** behaviour. They say we must treat all individuals in the same way. Everyone is equal because everyone is a human being. No one gets special treatment. Let's imagine a scenario where you might have to put this to the test.

CASE STUDY

There are two people drowning in the river. One is your friend Liz, and the other is a famous brain surgeon (here he is again!). Your friend is a shop assistant. What should you do?

Kant offers us no help. It's our duty to save lives. But there's only one lifebelt. A Utilitarian would, I'm afraid, recommend that we save the brain surgeon. He will save hundreds of future lives, and that will produce a lot of happiness. Your friend Liz, well, she helps people to buy nice clothes, but it's not like she's going to save many lives. It's not much of a contest.

But friends are special to us. We'd probably throw the lifebelt to Liz and hope that the surgeon was a good swimmer. Friendship makes us **subjective** and **partial**, and we don't think much about 'ends' when we see our friends in trouble. We feel obligated to them in ways that are not necessarily moral. So is there something wrong with us, or with these moral systems?

Here are some more questions and possible responses on friendship.

 Some of the holiest of the Christian saints were friendless hermits. Were they good men?

R Can hermits be good? Yes, say Christians. They get closer to God. No, says Aristotle. They can't possibly flourish in the absence of all human company.

Q Is it only human to feel resentment at a friend's success? Or would you never feel that way?

R We're all sometimes envious of a friend's success. But it's not something we should be proud of. Try to suppress it and be glad for your friend. He might take you out for dinner to celebrate.

Q Do you feel that your friends have changed your tastes, values or beliefs in some way? Have these changes made you a more interesting person? How?

R I have been changed by my friends. I listen to jazz music with more enjoyment. I know more about archaeology. I bought a bicycle, and fully intend to ride it more. I'm learning to play the ukulele. Thanks, guys.

Q How many friends would you forgive if they rang you up at 3.00am?

R There are about three friends I could forgive if they rang me at 3.00am. How about you?

Q 'I don't really feel I'm part of a community. I hardly know anyone who lives round here. My community is my friends.' Do you feel like this? Is there anything wrong about it? Could you do anything to change it? Would it be worth your while?

R A lot of people now think of their 'community' as non-geographical. But that doesn't mean that you can't be neighbourly as well. Good neighbours can become good friends, according to a popular Australian soap.

Q Are Facebook friends real friends? How many Facebook friends do you have? How many close friends? Are they different? How?

R Some young people I know have 500 or more Facebook 'friends', which seems a bit odd to me. How can you possibly form deep and lasting relationships with so many people? Isn't Facebook devaluing the word 'friendship' rather? It might be better to think of Facebook friends as 'acquaintances' perhaps. Nothing wrong with that, in theory, but in practice it might offend some individuals who overestimate your feelings for them. I can see the problem. Plato thought that you have to meet friends face to face and engage with them in all sorts of ways: physical exercise, games, political discussion, drinking and laughing. I sort of agree. But then I've only got seven

Facebook friends and perhaps I'm just jealous. And Plato didn't have broadband, after all. Nevertheless, it seems to me that real physical friends that you can touch are more valuable than ones you can only make contact with electronically.

 You need friends.

10. Romantic love

Love is important (but not very philosophical)

Most of us fall in love at some time or other, and there are innumerable novels, plays, songs and poems about the triumphs and tragedies of it all. Love is very important to us – it determines how we think and behave. It has a large say in who we are and who we become. Some say it has a spiritual and ethical element that simple lust lacks.

How do we know when we're in love? It's an emotion that seems self-evident to us. But it's a private phenomenon, not something we can describe literally or explain clearly. How could it ever be made logical, proved or disproved, made moral or immoral? All's fair in love and war, after all. You can see why it's a problem for philosophers.

Courtship and culture

There are many unwritten cultural rules governing romance. Traditionally, love involves an active man 'courting' a woman who initially feigns indifference. This makes courtship a minefield of potential misunderstandings and embarrassment. Women supposedly exist in a state of passive 'readiness' although they can often give their chosen young man a friendly nudge or two.

Love can also be instantaneous. Many young men still maintain that they intuitively 'knew' straight away that they would eventually marry that girl they saw 'across a crowded room'.

Q Do you believe in love at first sight?

R Infatuation and lust at first sight is one thing. Love seems to be something else.

Q Can you ever choose to be in love?

R Love doesn't seem to be something that you can choose. It would be like choosing a belief. You either believe or you don't. It's an involuntary affair.

Love can also become obsessive, a kind of illness. Love can be immensely destructive. It can destroy marriages, damage children, lead to suicidal despair. Go to the opera and see.

So romantic love is still partly 'cultural', and society still frowns on promiscuous women, because society remains patriarchal – men have more economic and political power. But many women now are economically independent and less cowed by male expectations. Bold girls ask boys out on dates and don't expect to receive long poems devoted to their purity and beauty. We have more freedom, more partners, so we learn more about power, insecurity, and the complexities of relationships. But unrequited love can still feel pretty awful.

Is love just physical?

As well as being partly cultural, romantic love is obviously also very 'natural'. Sexual desire is something inbuilt, as natural a drive as hunger or thirst.

 Falling in love produces major chemical events in our bodies that stimulate the brain's pleasure centres to make us happy and excited, even slightly mad. This is because nature wants us to perpetuate our genes and mix them up, and falling in love is the beginning of this process. Men generally look for partners who are young and beautiful, and women like men who are handsome. But women are also looking for security, status and reliability. They need partners who will protect them and their mutual offspring until their own children are potential parents. This may be why women are, superficially anyway, more reluctant to have relationships with many men, and men are more promiscuous.

But there's more to love than mere procreation. People gravitate towards each other for all sorts of reasons:

compassion, friendship, sympathy, a wish to belong, fear of loneliness, feelings of insecurity and inferiority, egotism and other feelings, both good and bad.

Mature love – the end of romance?

It's difficult to know how much culture or nature determines men's and women's romantic behaviour – because it's a confusing muddle of both. Romantic love is a complicated mix of powerful innate drives and social, cultural and historical conventions that still channel our instincts into codes of behaviour that society prefers.

Q Is there any way of telling whether a relationship will last?

R How can you possibly tell whether a relationship will last? Like most things in life, it's a gamble. But many of us have been physically attracted to someone whom we subsequently found to be dull, irritable, trivial, obsessive, or merely unpleasant. So it's a good idea to think about character as well as looks. There's more to love in the long term than infatuation.

If we're like most people, then passion will eventually become a less urgent affair, still 'romantic' but also more conscious and less determined by physical desires. Our relationship will be moderated by mutual respect and empathy. Both parties realize that it's wise to let their partners be themselves and not some idealized better half. It sounds duller, but it has its merits. There's more openness perhaps, and more negotiation. This may be a good thing, it may not. It may make us happy and content, it may not. It will depend on the people involved.

Q Lovers can't be friends. Do you agree?

R This is a rather cynical view of love. It implies that lovers don't really know much about each other and don't go in for all the things mentioned in the previous chapter on friendship, like trust, sharing, commitment and flourishing. Love does seem more volatile and dangerous than friendship, though, especially in its early stages.

The pessimistic philosopher Arthur Schopenhauer (1788–1860) thought that romantic love would often end badly, regardless of who we are. At the time, we all think that there's nothing more important than love. It will make us happy for ever. But, alas, says Schopenhauer, love is merely nature's trick to get us to procreate. We think that there's more to it than that, but there isn't. We fall in love with people who, subconsciously, we believe will smooth out all of our bad qualities when we have children. I'm tall and have a big nose, so I will look for someone smaller with a small nose. And when we've had children and raised them, well, that's us finished with. Why should an involuntary biological drive have anything to do with our own personal happiness?

Father of psychoanalysis Sigmund Freud (1856–1939) agreed with much of this and thought that being married came with a high price tag. We have to suppress our more irrational and destructive desires in order to live in an orderly and rational society. This can keep us safe, but it may also make us miserable.

Love and the philosophers

Some philosophers have asked if romantic love makes you a better person.

THINK ABOUT IT When we are loved we feel valued and special. We like ourselves more, we become more confident. Love may begin with storms of uncontrollable emotion, but it can, eventually, be good for us, even make us better people. Perhaps. But love also interferes with the autonomy of individuals. When we're desperately in love, we're less 'free'. So does that make love a bad thing?

Socrates thought that sexual passion was something we share with animals, and so of little worth. Love was no more than a rather inferior response to an individual's physical beauty. Fortunately this develops into a more spiritual awareness of someone's soul, and finally an appreciation of 'Beauty' itself. Socrates doesn't have much to say about sharing or companionship, though. In Plato's *Symposium* (a kind of drinks party and talking shop) Aristophanes suggests that lovers were, in a previous life, one hermaphroditic person, which explains why they're so happy to be reunited, returning to a single, shared mystical soul.

This idea of a 'union of souls' is common. Somehow two different people become a new entity, one person. Distinctions between your interests and my interests become blurred. Love involves a sharing of identity, emotions, values and beliefs. It offers an escape from the isolation and loneliness of the self that most of us feel some of the time. So we allow another person to change us in all sorts of ways. It's powerful stuff, love. This is why, when a relationship ends, a lot of people feel that they have lost an important part of themselves.

Love and empathy

A mutual life inevitably involves a certain loss of freedom, a greater degree of compromise, decisions becoming shared. This new blurring of identity worries some philosophers. The loss of independence and individual uniqueness seems too high a price to pay. It's as if one person is 'colonizing' another.

REMEMBER THIS!!! Other philosophers point out that a close union may instead lead to a greater degree of empathy. **Identifying totally with someone else and making the effort of the imagination that this requires is a key component of moral goodness.** By identifying with one other person we subsequently learn how to identify with many others. We become more understanding and much kinder. Romantic love eventually makes us happier, more sociable and so better citizens.

Aristotle thought that love and marriage form a platform for our ultimate aim of flourishing. Even Schopenhauer thought that it was the illusion of romantic love that prevented many of us from behaving badly.

Reciprocity

Some philosophers think that this notion of a union of two souls is too mystical or even undesirable. Who wants to be no more than a part of someone else? Surely love is just mutually beneficial? You identify with your partner when they're happy or sad, disappointed or elated, but you and they remain separate entities. This sounds more down-to-earth and sensible, but that doesn't mean it's a better way of defining love.

A romantic partnership may also be unequal. It's not always easy to recognize the difference between concern and domination. Aristotle thought that a relationship could become distorted when one person was ruled over by the other or the love was too one-sided. Relationships can easily become unequal. True love should be reciprocal, but between equals.

 Can you fall in love with someone you don't trust?

R I think you probably can. But it might be unwise.

Love improves you

Those of us who have been in love probably feel that someone who has never experienced love is somehow diminished – but then perhaps they can also cope with loneliness better than we can.

Q Does love make you more, or less, selfish?

R Sometimes love makes you selfish, sometimes it makes you more generous. I don't think there's an answer to this question. Do you?

Aristotle thought that love gave us a better sense of ourselves: our partners can be more objective about us and so helpful to us – wiser about us than we are ourselves. This may be true, but love can also be a kind of 'mutual egoism' – lovers like to tell each other how beautiful and intelligent they are, after all. Why would such a gorgeous and clever person choose you? Well, obviously, because you're a paragon of wonderfulness yourself!

So who's going to tell you the objective truth? Perhaps your lover, who has your best interests at heart? Or perhaps not your lover, worried about damaging the eggshell of your frail little ego. Better to ask people who don't love you. They may give you better advice and point out your moral failings.

But that's enough cynicism. Love may not make us wiser or better people. Most of us still want to believe that being loved increases our sense of well-being, reduces stress, increases our longevity, and adds our little world of happiness to those huge sums that Jeremy Bentham spoke about. And it's not something that's ever going to disappear from human life. So good luck. I hope you have found, or will find, 'the real thing'.

 Love is good for you, if you're lucky.

---

11. Being married

What is marriage?

A lot of people who fall in love eventually decide to have a wedding. It's understandable. It helps join families together. It makes a private relationship public. And it's good to dress up and be the centre of attention for a day.

But we all know that there's more to getting married than frocks and flowers. That's because marriage is a social institution. It regulates sexuality, procreation and child-rearing. Many philosophers and politicians approve of it because they believe that it produces happiness and stability. Marriage is also a legal contract, a social practice and, very often, a religious rite. In the past, marriage had more to do with economics and politics than love. Nowadays we like to think that two people have to be in love if they are to marry. It may even make them into 'good persons'.

The philosophers

Like romance, marriage is a lot of interrelated things rather than one big, obvious thing. Philosophers have rarely agreed about its benefits.

- Aristotle was in favour, because, like many politicians today, he thought the 'hard-working family' was one of the essential building blocks of the state. Sexual stability produces stable societies.

- Early Christians like St Paul insisted that sex should take place only between married individuals, and even then he wasn't too happy about it.

- Kant thought that marriage involved two people treating each other as ends and not means, and so was a good thing.

- Kierkegaard disagreed – he thought that romantic love and marriage are incompatible.

- Hobbes and Locke thought that marriage could never be between equals because men are stronger – in all sorts of ways. So women marry for protection.

- John Stuart Mill believed that most marriages made women inferior and treated them like slaves, and marriage survived only because men benefited from it.

- Karl Marx thought that the purpose of marriage was to convert women into private 'property' and give men a way of controlling reproduction – a man needs to be sure it's his own children who inherit.

The odd contract

Most people nowadays think that marriage has to be between two equals. It's a sort of contract between them: to avoid promiscuity, look after each other and share child-rearing. But if it is a contract, it's a very odd one.

THINK ABOUT IT

Normally contracts are voluntarily drawn up only by the individuals concerned and can be dissolved at any time, by mutual consent. Marriage isn't like that. It's more like a contract between two individuals and the institution of marriage itself. It supposedly lasts until the death of one partner. But is it really possible for someone to promise to love someone else for ever? Do we actually have that sort of rational control over our future feelings?

Nowadays the marriage contract is more flexible – people sign pre-nuptial agreements and have 'no fault' divorces. But it's still a very strange contract. If it were to be specifically tailored for the two individuals involved, then it would become more like a business arrangement than a law. The state wouldn't approve – it prefers marital agreements to be legal, unambiguous and universal so that the laws of taxation, inheritance and benefits can be applied fairly.

Privatized marriage

But why have this contract at all? Why can't two individuals decide for themselves how to live their lives? Why don't we just privatize marriage? The state might reply that marriage needs some kind of legal back-up. It's a tradition with a long and successful history. It encourages self-control, is vital for child-rearing, and, on balance, produces greater amounts of happiness and fulfilment in the lives of its citizens. But what about marriages that are childless, and what about civil partnerships? The marriage contract is unique. After all, the state has nothing to say about individuals and friendship. No one in a liberal and pluralist society thinks that it's the state's job to interfere with our private desires, choices and lives. Perhaps, one day, we will think the same way about the state and marriage.

Q Who benefits more from marriage – men or women?

R Men do, according to numerous opinion polls. But we're dealing in averages and generalities here.

Women and marriage

The legal status of matrimony hasn't done women any favours in the past. Women gave up most of their legal rights as soon as they said 'I do'. Their property became their husband's. They weren't allowed to sign contracts, they couldn't complain about being attacked by their spouses, and so on. Marriage didn't usually protect them at all, but made them more vulnerable to abuse and injustice. Men liked to explain how it was 'natural' for women to obey their husbands, be monogamous and benefit from male protection. Marriage was a private matter. This 'liberal' view of the relationship between the government and the individual sounds admirable. The trouble is that it leaves married women without much protection from bad or lazy husbands. Women still contribute more to domestic work than men. They are responsible for most of the childcare, whether they work or not. If marriage were abolished, then perhaps women would have rather different views about their economic independence and might flourish in a different way.

Q a) Marriage should be a private matter between two people only; b) Marriage is a public declaration and involves families and the state as well as the two partners. Which of these two statements is nearer to the truth? Which one do you agree with more?

R Is marriage a private or a public agreement? At the moment it's a public affair. The state will insist that you obey certain laws from now on. You can't marry more than one wife or husband, for example. If marriage were to become a wholly private concern, then this would create huge problems for the state and the legal system.

Staying married

In spite of all this, most people are optimistic about their chances, even though the number of people who decide against getting married is on the increase. So how come some people stay married for long periods of time? It's helpful to be perceptive from day one. Too many individuals think their partner will miraculously change when they are married. Their partner will abandon his frog nature and become a prince, but, alas, the truth is he will probably remain just as croaky and amphibious. There's also quite a lot of luck involved, or, if you're a cynic, inertia.

Q Is divorce too easy these days? Should it be made harder? Should it be made easier? Are the present levels of divorce acceptable or unacceptable?

R It seems stupid and wicked to force two people to remain in a relationship that both wish to abandon. But it's vital that children are protected from any emotional and financial damage that ensues.

Like friendship, marriage requires a lot of work. It helps if you begin with the assumption that your marriage is permanent. You have to be flexible and willing to change. You have to give each other privacy. But you should also enjoy your partner's company and be prepared for a lot of talking, arguing and listening. After a while you will build up a kind of private language of jokes and references to mutual history.

CASE STUDY

Rufus goes out with some old friends, and they end up drinking at a hotel on the outskirts of town. He goes to the bar to buy his round when he glances into the hotel lounge. He's surprised to see the wife of one of his friends in a passionate embrace with a man who's clearly not her husband. What does he do? Does he keep quiet or tell his friend what he saw?

Rufus is in a quandary. And so am I. There are a lot of unknowns here. Did he see a moment of madness or a long-standing relationship? Do his friend and his wife have an 'understanding' about extra-marital affairs? Her husband may not want to know about his wife's infidelities. Rufus has to try to guess what his friend's wishes are. But if he isn't sure, then I think I'd advise him to remain silent.

Gay marriage

Gay men and women may be in a dilemma. They think they should be able to marry. But if they do, aren't they simply yearning to be 'normal' like heterosexuals? Marriage may make their relationship legitimate in the eyes of the state. They get more rights – like those governing inheritance, tax, custody and immigration. But some gay writers insist that same-sex relationships are less possessive and more diverse than heterosexual ones. The right of gay people to marry might be fairer, but it may not make them happier or more fulfilled.

Q Do you agree that gay people should be allowed to marry? Why? (Or why not?)

R There's no rational reason to exclude gay people from marrying. Why should they be excluded? They are tax-paying citizens, after all.

Just married

So now the wedding's over. The honeymoon is a distant memory. You've just read what the philosophers have to say about marriage. Do you feel depressed? Informed? Wiser? Angry? Do you wish that you hadn't read any of it? Philosophers generally think that the more you know, the more mature you will be, and the more fulfilled you will end up. You have to decide for yourself, I'm afraid. Just think a bit before you make, or agree to, that proposal.

And as to whether marriage will make you a better person or not, that's really up to both of you.

 It's not just your partner you're getting married to.

---

12. Being a parent

The reality

Becoming a parent changes a relationship for good. Suddenly there are three people involved and not two. You don't get enough sleep. Your living quarters get messier. You have to learn to multi-task. Childcare will take up more hours of your day. It's relentless. It helps if you've already looked ahead and worked out a different attitude to time and work. And you'd better learn a bit more about babies. They're determined egotists who need a lot of feeding, panic when their routines are changed, and cry a lot.

Q What fundamental obligations do you think you have as a parent towards a child? What are the ones the state should insist on?

R Most parents would say that they have to provide children with safety, food, shelter, warmth, affection, an education, financial support and moral advice, when asked for.

Children and the state

Philosophers don't usually concern themselves much with the grubbier practicalities of childcare. Jean-Jacques Rousseau famously praised the innocence and wisdom of children, but then gave all his to a local orphanage. Philosophers are more interested in analysing concepts and thinking about rights than warming feeding bottles. So what are the rights of children and parents and society? (Notice how that last word crept in.) What are the rights of the child?

Most philosophers think that parents shouldn't indoctrinate children too much, although many do. Philosophers like to talk about the 'autonomy of the child'. So, in an ideal world, children would be allowed to think for themselves as much as was practically possible. Not an easy road for parents to go down. Parents are also obliged to reorder their own lives to some extent so that they cater for the needs of a child. And they have a special kind of authority over the child, as does society. So suddenly there are two new relationships in your life. One with the child and yet another one with the state. This means that parents are more like 'trustees' than 'owners'. Children aren't the same as slaves or golden retrievers.

Q Children need to be educated. But about what? If parents have a duty to educate their children, what sorts of things should they tell them about? My friend Liz says that parents are obliged only to feed, clothe, love their kids and tell them what the 'house rules' are. Is she a good or a neglectful parent?

R I think Liz has got parenting about right. I think that she should teach her children the Highway Code and some elementary moral rules. After that it would be information on request.

 My friends Jake and Anna are 'parachute parents'. They're determined that their son Martin will have the best possible start in life. He's about to go to secondary school and has been offered a place at the school nearby. But they want him to go to a better school further out, in the suburbs. They tell the education authorities that the family all live at Anna's mother's house which is in the catchment area of the other school. It works. Martin goes to his new school and is happy there. He's doing well. Everyone is pleased. Did my friends do anything seriously wicked?

Did Jake and Anna do the right thing? The answer is no, I'm afraid. What they did was fraudulent and illegal. By taking a place in the school that isn't theirs by right, they may have excluded another student who does qualify to go there. What they can do is lobby local councillors and the education authority about their local school, become governors of the school, or pay for a private tutor. It's understandable when parents want the best for their child, but it's wrong to cheat the system in this way.

Responsibilities

Society would like you to raise good citizens and literate workers. So you can't remove your child from school without making some prior arrangements. The upbringing is now shared between you and society. As a parent the state insists that you have responsibilities and duties towards the child. You have to feed, clothe, shelter, nurture and protect your offspring. The state won't allow you to force your child to go up chimneys for cash or go without medical care. (It doesn't prosecute you, though, if you allow your child to become horribly obese.)

 My friends Joel and Mary are lovely old hippies who can be a bit weird. When I went to see them last year I was a bit startled when I talked to two of their kids. They clearly believed totally in UFOs, ghosts, reincarnation and crop circles (made by extraterrestrials). Their mum and dad had told them all this stuff. What do you think? Do you think their parents are harmless? Should they tell their children this nonsense, as if it were all true? Does the state have any right to interfere with how these two are bringing up their own children?

Teaching silly nonsense to children seems harmless enough. We tell children about Santa Claus and see no harm in it. Many parents instruct their children in religious beliefs of all kinds which are equally unprovable. But it would be better for Joel and Mary to discuss their beliefs openly with their children, and explain what others say as well. On the whole, though, imposing dogmas of all kinds onto children seems wicked to me.

Whose child?

Most philosophical talk about parents and children focuses on procreation. This is partly because science has dreamed up all sorts of new ways to make and incubate babies. So what makes a parent? The obvious answer is the biological one – the DNA from the parents. And some say that because you 'own' the DNA then you also 'own' the child. But thinking of children as property doesn't help clarify things very much. Children sort of 'own' themselves really. They're ends, not means. But if a woman uses a donated egg because she has none of her own, who is the mother? Most people would say the pregnant woman is the mother. She went through all of the discomfort and risk of becoming pregnant, the child was a part of her for nine months and has now bonded with her. Fine.

But what about a surrogate mother who has rented out her womb to a fertilized egg for nine months? Is she allowed to claim the child as hers and break the contract she originally made with the client-parents? Should such a contract be legally enforceable? This is where philosophers get a bit stumped. Is surrogacy a bit like babysitting someone else's child, or is it more like handing over your own child? You can say that the couple 'intended' to plan for and have and raise the child, so it's theirs. Or you can say that they 'caused' the child to exist. But neither of these arguments is very convincing. Modern science has left us with some very problematic moral questions.

Q Some people think that employing a surrogate mother to give birth to 'your' child is fine. If she's willing and gets paid, where's the problem? Other people say that surrogacy is wrong because it's unnatural and is usually exploitative – rich would-be parents exploiting poor and desperate women. What do you think?

R Surrogacy is a difficult moral issue. There may be an element of exploitation involved. But then being childless can be a devastating condition for some couples. You could do some complicated 'happiness sums' for each individual and society in general. Whether you'd end up with a 'correct' moral solution is doubtful, though.

The right to breed

Do two adults have the right to procreate in the first place? To some this seems like an absurd question. Making babies is what most of us do. What business is it of the state to interfere? Once government is allowed to interfere with our private family lives then it may lead to all sorts of horrors like licences to breed – so that having children becomes a privilege rather than a right.

But perhaps the state should insist that having children also involves certain conditions. Parents should have to prove that they can at least provide safety, food, shelter, education, medical care and affection. And should we allow very young people or very old people to be parents?

It's not easy. Is having children a right? 'Rights talk' like this doesn't usually make things clearer. Most of us assume that we have a 'natural right' to have children, perhaps because we're programmed by nature to produce them. But maybe our society also has the right to manage the size of its population. So which right is more important?

A Utilitarian might be able to calculate how much happiness and misery is normally experienced by 16- or 60-year-old parents and their children. They might then recommend that it's wiser to have children when you're more mature but still resilient enough to cope. However, most of us would be against governments denying the right of the poor to have kids, or insisting on compulsory abortions.

Q The world is overpopulated. Resources are getting scarcer. China insists that couples should only ever have one child. Should we have the same legislation here? If we did, what would be the problems?

R The world is undoubtedly crowded. Its resources are finite and shrinking. But should we give the state the power to interfere with individual private lives so drastically? Perhaps instead we should educate people to think very hard about having more than two children.

Science and babies

Most people think that couples have the right to have babies. But science is moving so fast. If science eventually allows parents to choose the gender of their babies, or even to clone children, then our moral alarm bells will start ringing. It may not be a good idea for mothers to have lots of babies through IVF methods or for them to produce only male children. At present we allow parents to choose the gender of their child if there's a good medical reason, but not as a matter of preference. We don't want a society with a huge gender imbalance, and we don't want to encourage unspoken sexist ideas about 'good' and unwanted babies either.

But in the near future it may well be possible to make babies that are highly intelligent, healthy and attractive, by screening or by DNA splicing. We don't object to parents fast-tracking their children by paying for extra tuition, so why should we object to this kind of choice? A Utilitarian would see the happiness of parents, the child itself and the benefits to society as a whole. But they would also have to think about a future society with two classes – the clever and beautiful and the ugly and stupid. Would this be a desirable or happy society? The moral confusion is just beginning.

Making and having children is now ethically rather more complicated than it was.

Q It won't be long before we will be able to manipulate parental DNA so that all babies are born to be highly intelligent. This pleases some people and horrifies others. What's your view?

R 'Intelligence' comes in all shapes and sizes. We will still need intelligent carpenters and binmen as well as philosophers and investment bankers. In our meritocratic society, the race to the top now seems to produce more and more inequality. An artificially enhanced elite would produce even more economic and political disharmony.

 There's more to having children than you think.

131

13. Growing up

Children and philosophers

The most important thing that philosophers have to say about children is pretty obvious to most parents: *children are different*. The child psychologist Jean Piaget (1896–1980) found that children conceive the world very differently from adults. They tend to be 'animists' when little – anything that moves is somehow 'alive'. They live in a different world, they have a different consciousness. Children also ask questions that seem, on the surface, to be 'philosophical'. Are dreams real? How did everything begin? What is time?

'Childhood' itself is something that appears to be as much a cultural and historical phenomenon as a natural one:

- Medieval peasants had a very different understanding of childhood to that of Victorian middle-class parents.
- Nineteenth-century Romantic poets suggested that children were more innocent, even wiser in some ways, than adults.
- Plato and Descartes thought that children were born with a large amount of innate knowledge. They already knew some basic mathematics and morality, as soon as they were born.
- Locke, on the other hand, thought that children knew absolutely nothing at birth – all their knowledge was acquired from experiencing the world.

Moral development

But when do children start to become moral beings? There are many different philosophical opinions about human nature and how we develop morally. As we grow up, do we get better at being good?

THINK ABOUT IT

Parents who take a hard look at their own children don't see angels. They see selfish little egotists who have to be encouraged to share, to be honest and to restrain their violent tendencies. Most parents feel that they are qualified to do this demanding task of moral education. After all, their own sense of morality has improved over time. Their powers of conceptual analysis are greater. They can reason more effectively, and they have more experience of the world.

Sometimes this belief in personal moral progress is accompanied by a confident belief that society as a whole is improving. We no longer have public executions, put children down mines or have corporal punishment in schools. But, alas, when we look at how human beings have behaved in the last century, it's hard to be much of an optimist. If we're all getting morally better, how do we explain concentration camps, atomic bombs and racism? Horrible societies have found it all too easy to persuade the majority of their citizens to be horrible to minorities. It would be wonderful if we could educate children into becoming 'good persons', immune to vicious propaganda. But it wouldn't be an easy task.

How do we educate children to be moral without bullying them? Perhaps we have to start with children *as they are*. Children seem to have a natural need for social interaction with others, and that involves some degree of empathy and moral understanding. That's what Jean-Jacques Rousseau thought. So why do children grow up to be wicked? Why is there so much corruption and violence in the world? How does it get there? Rousseau thought it was obvious – children are socialized by societies that are corrupt and violent. Children like to imitate adults. We all eventually become habituated into badness.

KEY FIGURE Jean-Jacques Rousseau (1712–78) was born in Geneva but spent most of his life in France. There he met other French intellectuals who encouraged him to air his extraordinary and radical views on human nature, childhood, art, politics and society. He eventually changed European culture for ever – into something now called 'Romanticism'. Some people also think that his political ideas were responsible for the triumphs and the disasters of the French Revolution.

Rousseau's remedies for the evils of society were educational and political. If society is so bad, we either escape it or change it. So in his book *Émile* (1762) he described the education of a child raised in 'nature', away from society. Later on, he thought that society could be totally redesigned into small utopian city states of citizens who automatically always vote for the good of all. Alas, neither of these remedies seems very practical or desirable. We can't shut our children away from the world. We also live in imperfect and huge societies whose citizens are now counted in millions.

Aristotle wouldn't have understood Rousseau. How can society *always* be wicked? Society is what makes people human. Being a good person and citizen means repressing brutal instincts and nurturing good ones. All of us have the potential to become moral and happy human beings. We begin life as amoral infants. We are taught how to make moral decisions. We experience life and its complexities, we get into the habit of choosing a middle way. We become 'good persons' in both senses – moral and human. The two are inseparable.

Empirical investigations
Some psychologists have tried to investigate the moral development of children empirically (in other words, by experiment and observation), by asking children what they believe and by examining how they make moral decisions. They devise cunning questionnaires and simulation exercises to see if ethical reasoning does indeed develop as we grow older. What is going on in a child's mind as they

make moral choices? How much are they making these choices independently and how much are they influenced by others?

The psychologist Lawrence Kohlberg (1927–87) thought that moral development was a kind of hierarchical ladder with six rungs. He asked children of all ages to reason about problems involving fairness, justice, equality, loyalty, benevolence and various kinds of social welfare. He also looked at how children encouraged each other to cooperate and how they resolved conflicts. He was convinced that children were natural Kantians. So it's a very Kantian sort of progression which assumes that there's a kind of universal and objective morality that we all eventually come to share. Here are the six stages:

Stage One
Being wholly egotistical. Being moral means no more than being obedient because of the fear of punishment.

Stage Two
Conforming to the norms of a peer group, but for selfish reasons. At least recognizing that others have interests as well.

Stage Three
Being moral means being a 'good boy' and seeking the approval of others.

Stage Four

Being good means being loyal to authorities and social institutions. Doing what is right is what makes you a good citizen, a member of a group.

Stage Five

Believing that morality means obedience to the laws of the state because they are based on contractual agreements. Agreeing with Utilitarian views on happiness and democracy.

Stage Six

The belief in universal moral principles that override all other obligations, even society's laws, or empirical observations of 'happiness'.

So you begin as a selfish brat and, with time, you end up as Immanuel Kant. That's the idea. Kohlberg freely admitted that some adults never get much beyond stage three, and only a few ever reach the giddy Kantian heights of stage six. At each stage, the moral problems he set students got more complex. The best rejected Utilitarian morality because it can't guarantee a minimum degree of fairness, equality and justice to all.

Kohlberg was mostly interested in 'moral reasoning'. His six stages have little to do with the ability to empathize or show compassion. His tests for moral thinking are almost wholly about problem-solving. Virtue theorists would say that morality has far more to do with caring, benevolence, dialogue and relationships built up over time. Being moral implies negotiation, being tentative, recognizing that there are rarely simple solutions in life and being prepared to suspend judgement. To be fair, Kohlberg never said that the results of his research were conclusive. However, subsequent and more sophisticated experiments seem to show that Kohlberg's conclusions about moral development may well be about right.

Teaching goodness

Kohlberg's analysis of moral development can be useful for parents and teachers. Children already have their own rather simple understanding of morality, so it's best to try to build on that, rather than attempt to impose an incomprehensible 'higher' one. Simulation games exploring moral issues are one way of challenging children to think in new ways. Discussions and lessons that end in disagreement are often more interesting and useful than those that reach a happy consensus. But modern education is an ambivalent process. We encourage children to compete and then expect them to cooperate. We want them to obey teachers and then to think for themselves. But, if Aristotle is right, we shouldn't leave moral development to chance.

Q Can we really educate children into being good people?

R Well, we can probably point them in the right direction and encourage their good virtues, like cooperation and sharing. It's not a bad idea to teach by example. It's also fine to insist they obey a few elementary house rules. But when they reach adolescence the choices they make will be their own. Moral advice should then be provided only on request.

Education and morality

Politicians and parents, teachers and employers are always debating how 'useful' education should be. They're not usually talking about morality, though. Employers insist that education should be mostly vocational, in order to provide them with an efficient workforce. Teachers usually disagree – they think that there's something intrinsically good and beneficial about knowledge in itself. If we teach children a whole range of subjects then they will be able to think rationally and distinguish sense from nonsense. They also think that children should be encouraged to explore and discuss moral issues. We want well-informed and argumentative citizens who think for themselves, not obedient economic units whose sole purpose in life is to produce and consume.

Q 'I don't think schools should teach morals to children. That's the parents' job.' Do you agree?

R Parents are the primary influence on how children behave. But it's often hard to debate moral issues with your parents. So children need to debate moral issues with other children, in a controlled educational environment (in a classroom, with a teacher present to ensure fair play).

Schools and communities

In a Western liberal democracy we want children to grow up to make their own moral decisions. We don't believe in 'moral instruction'. We like to think that children are encouraged to be kind, cooperative and loyal – but then be allowed to make up their own minds about how to be happy. We want them to become independent citizens who determine the shape and direction of their own lives. This modern liberal ideology will often clash with the very different moral values and religious beliefs of some parents. They may want their children to be educated in a more traditional manner, into a specific culture. They are in favour of 'faith schools'. Their children become 'good persons' mostly because they are fully integrated members of their community. They share religious and moral beliefs. So who should decide what kind of morality children are taught – parents, teachers or politicians?

FAQ Should some religious communities have the right to teach their children in their own schools, or does this produce a more divided society?

I personally believe in the separation of religion from the state. But I can understand that some beleaguered minority groups want their own culture to survive. Nevertheless, there needs to be more integration between different groups, and faith schools seem to stand in the way of that happening. No one wants to live in a society of isolated ghettoes.

FAQ Should politicians have a say in the moral education of children?

I would say not, because they always have some kind of political ideology to impart, and what is taught will be constantly shifting, depending on who's in power. We want children to judge politicians, not politicians to indoctrinate children.

 Children are different.

14. Business

Business ethics

We live in a world of huge global corporations that have immense power over us. Public libraries are closing, unemployment is rising, benefits for the poor and the sick are being cut. All because some large banks miscalculated. They thought the good times would go on for ever. So are corporations like these wicked or just stupid? And what about the people in charge of them? Do they never get punished for doing bad and stupid things? What about the rights of individual employees? What if we think that the company we work for is covering up its wicked acts? Do we blow the whistle on them or stay loyal to our employer?

Q There are all sorts of laws governing what businesses can or can't do. But what about morality? Is there any room for morality in business?

R Yes. There has to be. For one thing, companies have to trust each other if they are to do business. A fraudster soon gets found out. Kant called business morality like this 'prudential' – a means to an end. Morality like this is just good for business, not a good in itself, and there are lots of companies that recognize morality only as effective PR. So it's wise to examine what they do, as well as what they say. An oil company might champion its environmental credentials while taking horrendous risks on its oil platforms. Clothes are cheaper than they used to be. Why? Because the people who produce these goods are badly underpaid and work long hours in sweatshops. It's easy to turn a blind eye to unpleasant facts, but not very ethical. Consumers don't realize how much power they have. If shoppers asked the right questions and acted according to the information they received, private companies would be forced to act more responsibly.

John sees some really cheap jeans in his local discount store. Then he remembers reading an article about this brand. They employ children in the developing world to make them – that's why they're cheap. Should he buy them?

I don't think that John should buy the jeans. He knows that they're cheap only because of the low wages of the kids that made them. If he buys them he's more or less endorsing the company's exploitation of poor children. The company might reply that they pay the standard wages of the country where their jeans are made. But I think they should provide a good example for others to follow, perhaps by building a school for the kids. They could explain this new policy to their customers. You never know, their ethical behaviour might be good for business.

Amorality in business and politics

A famous economist, Milton Friedman (1912–2006), insisted that businesses have to be amoral – their only 'moral' duty is to obey the law and pay dividends to shareholders. How they behave in other ways is entirely up to them. So if it's not actually illegal to pay starvation wages and spy on other companies, well, that's fine.

KEY FIGURE One philosopher who would probably have agreed with that was Niccolò Machiavelli (1469–1527). He lived at a time when Italy was a series of small city states often run by powerful individual families. Some of them, like the Borgias, were famous for their cruelty and general wickedness. Machiavelli was himself imprisoned for his 'betrayal' of the Medici family. So he knew quite a lot about power and politicians from personal experience. He thought that the study of politics could be made scientific. What he found was that, in political life, the end always justified the means. In his book *The Prince*, he described how those in charge actually *do* behave, not how they *should*. Before then, practically all philosophical books were **normative** – they were about how people should behave. Machiavelli's book is **descriptive** – it just tells you what they do. Quite a few executives of large companies have admitted to reading *The Prince* with some enthusiasm. This is probably because it accords with many of their own business practices.

Machiavelli says that there's no place for traditional morality in politics or business. It would be impossible to run things if there were. So statesmen shouldn't tell the truth if it's advantageous to lie. If, as a politician, you want to cut wages, introduce new taxes and penalize the poor, fine, but appoint a deputy to do the dirty work. He'll get all the blame, not you. And when the period of austerity is over, sack him and step in as the people's saviour. Doing unpopular things and then becoming even more popular – who can argue with that? The well-being of the state is all that matters.

Many citizens agree with this approach. They think it's better to have a pragmatic, or even a wicked man in charge of things. That way the state is made secure and everyone enjoys peace and prosperity. When politicians get idealistic and moral, the results are often disastrous, in the form of misconceived 'crusades', bankruptcy, civil war or worse.

A lot of economists and politicians would still agree with much of this. In the past, perfectly respectable companies traded in slaves, sold opium to Chinese addicts and exploited colonized countries without a backward glance. Most corporate bosses still think that their main ethical purpose is to maximize profits and pay shareholders. This often involves complicated tax avoidance strategies, industrial espionage, bribery and covert donations to dodgy politicians. Some of these activities are clearly immoral, others less so. It's getting hard to tell.

Business is good

Let's not be too cynical. It's time to defend business a bit. From a Utilitarian standpoint, commercial activity is good – it increases financial growth and consumption. Businesses provide more goods and services. More people get wages, savings grow, governments receive more taxes and public welfare benefits. Thanks to business, a larger number of citizens, rich and poor, get greater amounts of material happiness. This is even true for people in developing countries – workers are paid wages, however small, exports bring small profits and, very slowly, everyone's standard of living is raised slightly, as they join the global economy.

We just have to acknowledge that business will always be competitive and driven by the profit motive. The fittest will survive and the weak will go to the wall. And business does adhere to a contractual, pragmatic morality. People can't trade if there's no trust or honesty. Even so, there's still plenty of wriggle room left for creative accounting, insider trading, excessive executive rewards and a bit of undisclosed bribery. Business is business.

Q 'Don't criticize business. It's firms like ours that produce wealth. We pay wages and taxes. If we don't cut a few moral corners, then we won't be successful. No more jobs, schools and hospitals. Grow up! This is the real world we're living in.' Do you have any sympathy for this view?

R I can sympathize with this businessman to a certain degree. Global competition is fierce and often ruthless. But it doesn't follow from this that businesses always have to cut moral corners. More and more, businesses are judged on how they act as well as by what they say. Consumers like to buy products and services that don't damage the environment or exploit people. They want their purchases to be 'guilt free'. So 'moral' businesses may eventually become more profitable. It's also true that business creates wealth – and not just for the top people. Government spending does indeed come partly from taxation on private companies. And governments do a lot to encourage economic growth. But sooner or later private enterprise and governments are going to have to work out how to invent a new kind of capitalist economy that is static or even shrinking. Growth can't continue for ever. The world's resources are finite.

The workers

How a business treats its workforce is another moral issue. Many large corporations treat their workers purely as a means – to produce greater profits. This doesn't mean that their employees are treated badly – it's not sensible to exploit your sweatshop workforce to the point of utter exhaustion. Nevertheless, workers are always more vulnerable and expendable than employers. They have to fight and negotiate hard. They have to rely on governments to pass laws to protect them. And they don't always just want a bigger wage packet. They want to be treated fairly. This can mean a right to privacy – not to be spied on by CCTV all day, not to have their work monitored by computers, not to be tested for drug dependency, and so on. It can mean the right not to be discriminated against because of race, gender, sexuality, pregnancy, age, religion or disability.

Some employees would also like more say in how the company is organized and so demand more democracy in the workplace. If they have a say, then they become more like participants and less like paid slaves. They can flourish more. (In contrast, Marx thought that all workers would always feel alienated when working for their capitalist employers – they work hard but have only a very limited say.)

Q How much say should ordinary workers have in the affairs of the company they work for?

R People like to be treated as ends and not means. They feel they should have a say in how they are treated as a workforce. It helps if the company they work for explains the thinking behind important decisions or changes being made. Some companies make their staff shareholders, with the result that the workforce show a greater sense of commitment to their firm. Some businesses are entirely democratic, the whole workforce having a say on company policy. It's not necessary to treat employees as slaves. It's also probably bad for business.

Whistle-blowing

An employee sees something dishonest or illegal going on in their government department or private company. It could be fraud, corruption or a violation of health and safety legislation. They have evidence of the wrongdoing, they are impartial, and they think there's a threat of harm to others. They have tried to tell their managers of their concerns but have been ignored. Most of us would think that they are now entitled to tell the media, lawyers or the relevant authorities about what they've seen. The loyalty they owe to their employer is trumped by their moral concerns.

Aristotle would say that a good person has integrity and courage. Kant tells us that one of our main duties is to tell the truth. Utilitarians insist that we must try to maximize happiness and minimize suffering. So we'd have to blow the whistle. Soldiers need to be protected from bad equipment, airline pilots shouldn't be overworked, medicines should be safe. But beware. Whistle-blowers often face reprisals – they are sacked, demoted and ostracized by their colleagues.

 When would you 'blow the whistle' on your employer? When he told a few small lies to another firm or the tax man? When he inadvertently poisoned a local lake with some chemicals? When he sold some poorly made parts to a car manufacturer? When he ordered some workers to paint the roof of a house without using any scaffolding? (Let's assume that in all these cases you voiced your concerns to your employer and he told you to shut up or lose your job.)

R When would you blow the whistle on your employer? It would depend on how morally rigorous you want to be, and how much you value your job. It would also depend on how wicked the company and its bosses were. If your firm was quite deliberately endangering the lives of others for profit, then you would have to think very hard about your obligations to other human beings as well as your loyalty to your employer. Blowing the whistle to journalists or authorities isn't easy. It will not usually benefit the whistle-blower. But sometimes individuals feel that they have to act on their moral principles. **Being moral involves acting, not just thinking.**

Conclusions

Perhaps there should be some moral principles that all companies would be expected to share. No company should be allowed to exploit people, to be dishonest or to exploit a monopoly. Big, powerful companies shouldn't be allowed to force smaller ones into bankruptcy by dumping artificially cheap goods on the market. But most business-men and women will still say that they obey the law and that's all that should be required of them. Laws are obliga-tory and ethics often voluntary.

But consumers can be powerful too. If they are suspi-cious of GM foods, they won't buy them. They don't like to read about small children working a twenty-hour day either. So nowadays, big companies have some kind of 'ethical policy' – usually rather vague and often just window dress-ing. Some even have 'ethics officers' employed to monitor the company's ethical performance. But businesses won't change overnight. Most of them still think of ethics just as a set of rules. Perhaps it would be better if everyone thought of ethics as the way forward for all of us – busi-nessmen, advertisers and consumers – to flourish as wealth-generators, consumers and human beings.

Wendy goes to the supermarket. She sees an old man shoplifting food and putting it into his rucksack. Should she tell an employee?

This is a hard one. Wendy doesn't want to encourage crime, but nor does she want to see an old man locked up for stealing food. It's much easier to identify with a hungry old man than a huge retail corpora-tion. She's probably morally obliged to tell an employee, but I'd excuse her if she didn't. What do you think? What would you do if a checkout girl gave you £10 too much in your change? What would you do if a slot machine spat out two Mars bars instead of one?

---

15. Citizens or consumers?

It's always been difficult to be a good person. Never mind, says Aristotle, try harder next time. Don't beat yourself up about it. No one's perfect. It's the journey that counts. The more you try, the better you'll get. Unfortunately, we 21st-century people have new desires that can get in the way of flourishing. It's because we're all **consumers** now, more than we are **citizens**.

Modern Western society is based, to a large extent, on everyone's desire to purchase goods and services in ever-increasing quantities. We judge politicians on how effective they are in governing the economy and so satisfying our cravings for more. It hasn't always been this way. Our impoverished ancestors were happy if they had a roof over their heads and three meals a day. Nowadays, goods are far more plentiful and affordable. Everyone, even the very poor, now consumes more, and many traditional beliefs and values have changed for ever.

Q 'I shop therefore I am.' This is an ironic slogan invented by the modern artist Barbara Kruger (b. 1945). Does it make you laugh, annoy you, or just puzzle you?

R 'I shop therefore I am' is a sly reference to the bit of Descartes' philosophy that most people know: 'I think therefore I am.' (The one thing I can be 100 per cent certain about is that I'm thinking, and so therefore, someone's mind must exist, doing the thinking.) Thinking may be the most important thing about human beings. Aristotle certainly thought so. But is it true that thoughtless shopping defines us now? It's a slogan that should worry us and make us angry. None of us want to be defined as *just* consumers. It forces us to think about why the slogan is wrong, what it leaves out. What are the real things that make us truly successful as human beings?

'Affluenza'

The rich and famous benefit most from all this economic progress. They flaunt a lifestyle that we can read about in magazines. They look beautiful and own big houses and fast cars. They advertise and endorse particular products. Lots of us envy them and want to be like them, so we borrow and spend. We buy branded goods like cars and clothes, which we believe act as signals of our wealth and importance.

THINK ABOUT IT Advertising plays on our feelings of insecurity about who we are and where we belong. We want to be admired because of our wealth and possessions – these are primary values of a consumerist society, after all. But, however hard we try, we remain perpetually anxious, victims of **affluenza** and **status anxiety**.

Advertisers create a hyper-real world of beautiful people where only consumption can bring happiness. They make sure we associate certain products with those things that actually *do* bring us happiness – friends, family and good health. They even convince us that we're empowering ourselves if we buy what they're selling. So we think we're making free choices, but we aren't really. 'Our' desires are manufactured. Consumption becomes a way of life, an addiction. It becomes what we do and who we are.

Q Do you trust supermarkets? What techniques do they use to make you buy stuff?

R It would be unwise to be either totally cynical or naively optimistic about supermarkets. They want your money, not your well-being – though it's complicated, because your well-being (or your sense of it) may also help to make them money. They put the cheapest goods at the bottom of the shelves, they stigmatize their 'value range' with specially designed packaging (so everyone knows you're poor) while packaging their expensive 'upmarket' range more attractively. They also sell organic produce at inflated prices, put a premium on products that are 'good for you', and 'greenwash' products that aren't especially environmentally friendly. They play all sorts of tricks on you. Beware.

Consumer illness

Endless consumption doesn't actually bring us that much happiness. The more we try to keep up with other consumers, the more dissatisfied we feel. We need more and more, and we don't seem to be as happy as the advertisements promised. We get into debt, we get stressed through overwork, and we feel miserable.

This is partly the result of what philosophers call the **paradox of hedonism**. *The more we seek happiness, the more it eludes us.*

We all know that there's more to human beings than just consumption. We need relationships with others, creative activities, learning opportunities, maybe a simpler and more spiritual kind of existence. We can't buy these things in the high street or shopping mall.

Q Looking round your living room. How many of your possessions are crucial to your well-being, and how many aren't? Do a quick count, if you like.

R So how many of your possessions are vital? Everyone has a different answer to this one. Some of us live in a world of tidy, Scandinavian purity. Others, like me, live in a world of endless clutter. The Epicurean philosophers said that we must simplify our lives if we wish to be content. We need very few things to make us happy, they said. Make a list of all of the things you believe to be necessary to your well-being. When your list has more than 100 items on it, then perhaps you should think harder about the words 'necessary' and 'vital', and start again.

Anti-consumerism

Some people have begun to realize that owning more possessions doesn't bring happiness or contentment – especially now that incomes are shrinking and capitalism seems more vulnerable. So they're 'downsizing', buying locally produced goods, becoming more aware of their carbon footprint and trying to make their lives simpler.

My friend Pete is quite well off. He has a large house and a massive CD collection of obscure jazz music. He has several computers in the house and is a great blogger – about jazz mostly. His kids have both left home now and his wife is studying for a degree. But he says he's miserable. He yearns for a simpler way of life. He dreams of living in a caravan in Wales, learning how to play jazz guitar, raising goats and growing his own vegetables. Is he a wise man or an idiot? How would his life be different from what it is now? What might be tedious about his fantasy life? What would be good about it? He's been telling me about his dream now for years. So why doesn't he just go and live on the land? Would it would make him happier? What advice would you give him?

So what should Pete do? I told him not to sell his house but to rent a caravan for six months – three months in the summer and three in the winter. He could keep a few hens, start a vegetable garden, practise on his guitar in the cold winter months. His life would be different – quieter, less distracting, maybe boring. He might have to make more of his own music rather than just listening to others. The battle to stay warm could get tiresome. But he might become less stressed and more spiritual, and a much better musician. Whether his new life would make him happier or not would be up to him. It might be worth a try. His wife said she'd visit him once a month and bring him treats. But that was two years ago. He's still dreaming.

Some anti-consumer activists are attempting to wake us all from our consumerist slumbers. They institute an annual 'No Shopping Day'. They suggest we go for a walk or a bike ride instead. We all need to think about our consumerist society as a matter of urgency. We can't ignore the fact that the world's resources are finite. Sooner or later our children will have to adapt to a different kind of life where resources are scarce and everybody has to consume less. You never know – they might be happier.

 Shopping may not be the answer.

---

16. The good environmentalist

The planet and us

Until quite recently, being a good person was restricted to how you treated other people. Now it includes considering the interests of animals and the whole of the natural world. This is because we're beginning to see a great diminishing of biodiversity as all kinds of species die out. Our children are going to have to face the awful dangers of climate change. We have to think about the needs and interests of future generations. We're custodians rather than the owners of this planet. We don't want to leave our children a barren desert punctuated by junkyards of discarded cars and broken computers.

Q Do you think that everyone has to do their bit to save the planet? If you do, what does that mean? What should we do to help? What are you doing?

R How can we help to save the planet? There's not much we can do to stop Chinese factories belching out smoke, making things for us to consume – other than trying to consume less. But we can do practical things like recycling more, growing our own vegetables, shopping for local produce, using public transport, riding bicycles, voting

Green, and protesting against governments and corporations that pollute the environment.

Rights

We all think that human beings have 'natural rights' to food, clean water, shelter and respect, even if, in practice, many people don't actually have these things. Some of these rights have now been extended to animals and are backed by law so that they have become legal or 'positive' rights. This is partly because some philosophers like Tom Regan and Peter Singer have argued that animals 'count' morally: they are sentient beings like us – they can feel pain. So, in many countries it's now illegal to inflict unnecessary suffering on domestic pets and farm animals, although a lot will depend on what you mean by 'unnecessary' or 'suffering'. Ask battery hens, veal calves or animals used in medical research.

Q Should we make battery farming illegal? Would you be prepared to pay more for your eggs and chicken if you knew the hens were free-range?

R Should we make battery farming of hens, pigs, calves, all animals, illegal? Yes. Of course. We all know that it's cruel to imprison animals. How can they flourish in such conditions? If we're to make them a means to our ends, it should be done with respect. Battery farming should be stopped.

Most of us can see why animals count morally. But what about trees, woods, jungles, prairies, seas and glaciers? They don't feel pain and can't suffer. So how do they have moral rights? One way of approaching this dilemma is to point to the obvious fact that human beings don't exist outside of the natural world. We are part of a huge, complex ecological system, full of diversity, and perhaps that's what has moral worth.

 The scientist James Lovelock called this system **Gaia** – an ecological system of the organic and inorganic that is constantly striving for a kind of equilibrium. At the moment, human beings are a part of this system. We may not be so in the future. We may not even be that important for the planet's survival. A lot will depend on how we, as a species, behave over the rest of this century. It really is in our own interest to be more ecologically-minded.

People-centred environmentalism

The basis of most environmental ethics is that it's in our interests to protect the planet. The environment is useful or 'instrumental' to us, so we need to protect and conserve it because our very survival depends on it. This makes obvious sense. It's sometimes known as the **anthropocentric** or 'people-centred' approach, and it has forced some governments to take environmental issues far more seriously. It's just not in our interest to keep on burning fossil fuels and decimating rainforests. Rising temperatures and sea levels, floods and violent weather – all of these are bad for us.

Some people say that it's the job of governments to save the planet. What can they do? A lot more than they do now:

- They could fund a massive educational programme to explain why we should be more ecologially-minded.
- They could tax private cars according to how much they're driven.
- They could spend far more on public transport and make it easier to use.
- They could allow people to fly once a year and then tax them heavily if they wanted to fly again.
- They could make house insulation free.
- They could make allotments available to everybody so they can grow their own food.

You can add your own ideas.

Jennifer owns a 4x4 vehicle (or SUV, if you're American). It's big and uses lots of fuel. She says she needs it because sometimes the track to her house is covered in snow, and this vehicle doesn't skid. But the main reason she bought it is because she feels that she and her two young kids are safe in it. 'If I were ever in an accident, I know that I and the kids would probably be OK. They come first, I'm afraid. It's big and tough and solid. I paid for it with my money. It's not illegal to own one. I pay a huge amount of car tax and fuel tax. So who's business is it, other than mine?' Is she right?

Jennifer's vehicle does pollute the environment and contribute towards global warming, but then so do all petrol and diesel vehicles. Her excuse about the snow in the drive isn't very convincing if it happens only once or twice a year. The safety issue is more complicated. It seems to mean that rich people have a safety advantage over poorer citizens. There's some evidence to show that 4×4's are more dangerous than other cars in an accident: the ordinary car is demolished and the 4×4 is scratched. So the rich are more protected than the poor. But does that give the government the right to stop people buying what they want? It probably does, if what people buy is damaging the planet and jeopardizing all our futures. There's no easy solution, though. Perhaps these gas guzzlers should be taxed even more, and the money raised devoted to more road safety education and equipment.

Blindfolding ourselves

It's not going to be easy for us to change our ways. Religion and philosophy haven't always helped much. The book of Genesis insists that human beings were made in God's image and so have God-like powers over the whole of creation. '[They] have dominion over the fish of the seas and over the fowls of the air, and over every living thing that moveth upon the earth.' Aristotle thought that nature made all things specifically for the sake of Man. Kant thought that cruelty to animals was ill-advised, but only because it gave bad men a taste for cruelty.

THINK ABOUT IT Until recently, Western society has lived according to a kind of 'frontier ethics' – the belief that the world's resources are virtually limitless and that human ingenuity will always find solutions to problems of scarcity. Everyone assumed that population and economic growth could continue indefinitely. But endless growth is not sustainable. So being a good person now means taking this rather seriously.

Philosophies and the environment

For a Utilitarian, being a good environmentalist means that we have to extend our moral concern beyond ourselves, to animals and the whole of the natural world. This is a bit problematic. We need clothes, shoes, food and shelter – all resourced from our environment. Utilitarians would probably allow us to inflict damage on plants and maybe animals if such acts were necessary for our survival. But individual plants and even whole environments would still be of moral concern, not because they can experience 'happiness' but because they have 'interests' of various kinds, and because they're part of an ecological system. It's the whole that has moral worth.

A good Kantian might say that our environment must be treated as an end in itself, not as a means for satisfying our rapacious desires. A believer in Aristotelian virtue might extend the idea of 'flourishing' to all ecological systems that have the right to fulfil their destiny, just as we do.

FAQ Do we have moral obligations to people in the future, even though we'll never meet them?

The unsurprising answer seems to be yes. We would all feel a moral obligation to our great grandchildren, even though we might never meet them. We feel solidarity with starving people who are geographically remote from us, so why not people remote in time? Personally, I have an interest in the continuation of the human race. We are rather remarkable animals, after all.

The radicals

Radical ecologists insist that we have to change how we think about ourselves and our place in the world. They say that change has to be **psychological** and **conceptual**. For a long time now, human beings have thought of nature almost as if it were a machine governed by laws, to be exploited for human benefit. We also tend to think, because we're rational, that we're somehow 'outside' of the natural world. Our relationship with our planet has been disrupted. The radicals say we need a wholly new world view so that we think of nature as something with intrinsic worth. We might even have to return to the ways of our distant ancestors – living in small, self-sufficient communities again, rather than in cities.

My friend Jonathan is an environmental radical. He occasionally breaks the law by climbing up buildings and occupying government offices. He says the government should double the price of petrol. Everyone would use buses more, fares would get cheaper and cars would be used only for emergencies. He believes in a lot of other stuff too: insulation of all buildings should be free. There should be a massive advertising campaign about the dangers of global warming. Allotments should be made available to all. All food should be organic. People should be encouraged to be vegetarian. All energy should be generated from wind and wave power. 'I want my two kids to grow up safely', he says. Do you think he's very sensible or a bit of a nutter? Where do you agree with him and where don't you?

I agree with most of what he says. There are problems, though. If you try to control consumption by price, then only the poor suffer, which is unfair. The government might have to limit consumption by a kind of rationing. But that could lead to all sorts of other moral and political problems. Experience has shown that rationing goods and services is nearly always accompanied by a black market economy and a corrupt society. If politicians, rather than the market, decide on how to regulate the economy then the result is often shortages, waste and worse, an autocratic government. I suspect what we need to do is start by developing new (or older, pre-industrial) ways of thinking about ourselves and our environment.

The mystical view

The philosopher Benedictus Spinoza (1632–77) thought that everything in the world was somehow connected to everything else. Nature was us and we were nature, and a unique kind of holiness existed in all things. His 'natural spiritualism' influenced the philosopher Rousseau and some Romantic poets who believed that God was to be found everywhere in the natural world. Some ecologists now suggest that we should rediscover the **animistic** beliefs of our ancestors, who believed that all of the natural world was 'conscious' in some strange way. Nature was worshipped and respected for itself.

Well, perhaps nature *was* worshipped. And good luck to all tree-huggers everywhere. I don't personally think we have to worship trees to be ecologically moral. Some of these radical ideas make good sense to me, some don't. It seems obvious, though, that we have to think differently about ourselves and our planet, and sooner rather than later. The problem is that no one seems able to explain how we can persuade everyone else to think and behave differently. An awful lot of people rather like their cars, their central heating and their holidays abroad. But I guess we have to try. If we don't, then, eventually, there will be no 'good persons' left in the world. They will have died out, just like everyone else.

 We are a part of something bigger.

17. Fooling ourselves

Self-deception

We're self-deceived when we hold contradictory beliefs even though we've seen evidence that one of them is wrong. Many of us persuade ourselves to believe in something that, deep down, we know to be untrue. Sometimes we don't have much control over it, or we don't like to think about it too much. But is it *wrong*? Are we morally responsible when we deceive ourselves? Does it prevent us from being a good person?

Self-deception takes many forms. It seems odd – intentionally deceiving yourself and holding two mutually exclusive ideas in your mind. It's a kind of contradiction that seems to defy all that we know about logic, the mind and language. How can someone believe that homeopathy is good for you and not good for you, at the same time? Put like that, it seems impossible. But then human beings are illogical all the time. When I play ukulele with some degree of enthusiasm, I believe I'm amazing. When I think about it afterwards, though, I know I'm rubbish.

Q What sorts of things do you pretend to believe that you know, deep down, aren't true? (Facts about your age? Your appearance? Your intelligence? How much your friends think about you? How wonderful your children are?

How much you like your job? How successful you are? How moral you are?)

R I like to believe that I'm just a little over 21, liked by all, extremely gifted, and an extraordinary ukulele player. Alas, I'm none of these things.

More minds than one

One way of explaining self-deception is to say that the human mind isn't like a clear glass bowl, but more like a series of chambers, some hidden.

Psychoanalyst Sigmund Freud insisted that most of us are self-deceived in a more complicated way. He said that our minds are compartmentalized into that of which we're conscious and a darker, more mysterious place – the **subconscious**. The subconscious is full of irrational desires and fears where primitive drives force us to behave in ways that aren't chosen by our conscious selves. So the deceiving part of our minds operates at a lower level of consciousness and deceives the conscious part. Freud emphasized how irrational and emotional we are. We're full of desires, fears and anxieties that affect our beliefs and even cause them to contradict each other. A stalker harassing his victim will often insist that the more she tells him to get lost, the more she secretly loves him.

Am I responsible?

Self-deception often protects us from beliefs we don't want to face up to. But, all too often, self-deception also harms others. In Shakespeare's play, Othello persuades himself to believe in Iago's lies about his wife Desdemona, contrary to all the evidence. He becomes enraged to the point of madness and kills her. So sometimes not only is self-deception motivated by fear or jealousy, but it then makes these negative emotions even more intense.

FAQ Can self-deceivers be held responsible for what they do?

Most of the time the answer is yes. Lying to yourself is a kind of moral weakness, like cowardice or hypocrisy. Socrates thought that the most important moral task we all have is self-knowledge. Aristotle thought that self-deception was a bit like drunkenness – acceptable on the odd occasion but disastrous when it becomes a lifelong habit.

The more you engage in self-deception, the more you're blind to the evils of the world. For example, you might pretend to yourself that you're benefiting your workforce by employing them, and then ignore the dreadful conditions in your factories.

We all like to think well of ourselves but we can't make moral progress if we're morally blind. Self-deception implies a cavalier attitude to the truth. Kant thought it should be resisted at all cost. If we lie to ourselves, how can we examine our motives and do our moral duty? How will we realize that we're acting only out of self-interest? John Stuart Mill agreed – no one can apply the 'greatest happiness' principle conscientiously if they're liars to themselves.

THINK ABOUT IT

None of us is perfect. We're all self-deceivers. And sometimes our fear or anxiety is so great that we're simply unaware of how much we've deceived ourselves. We can condemn someone only if they actually *know* about the beliefs they're suppressing and have some control over them. But we still think it's unlikely that someone could be so self-deceived that they've forgotten all moral principles. Self-deception can often harm others, it undermines our free will, makes us credulous. It becomes a habit that gets worse. It prevents us from becoming 'authentic'. We all have a moral duty to examine our beliefs.

Is it always that bad?

I tell myself lies that I don't believe, every day. I still think I look quite handsome, in a dim light. Beliefs like these contradict what I know in the cold light of day, but they help keep me warm. Many of us quell our fears and anxieties by resisting, ignoring or pushing away frightening beliefs. Sometimes we're so successful at doing this that self-deception takes over completely and we no longer remember what it was that frightened us.

Q Which of *your* little lies are harmless, and which aren't? You might want to make a list.

R None of my small lies about being young, handsome, popular and musically gifted seems to be harmful to anyone other than myself. But it's probably immature, or even wrong, to fool myself too much. Being 'grown up' to some extent means facing up to unpleasant truths directly. Doing this should make me more resilient, more sympathetic to others, and might even make me practise the ukulele more.

But perhaps some kinds of self-deception are harmless or even beneficial. Maybe therapists should help us to forget and not face our fears? A degree of self-deception may even be necessary for our mental well-being. We shut out childhood traumas that return to us only in troubled dreams. Not many of us like to think about our own deaths. It's unsettling to remind ourselves that we live on a small planet in an impossibly huge and hostile universe. The useful fictions that we tell ourselves may not always be that wicked after all. It depends.

Collective self-deception: crowds

Collective self-deception can be much worse. Many people together can do more evil than one person. Groups, committees, companies and whole societies can all become self-deceived. Peer group pressure can be exceedingly powerful. It's usually easier to share other people's prejudices – you want to keep on cordial terms with them and you don't want to stand out and cause trouble. Sometimes this is harmless. Anyone who has been to a football match knows that crowds can be extraordinarily irrational. For the duration of the match, fans loudly remind each other that their team is the best in the world, when each individual knows that this isn't true.

Q Do you rather enjoy being in a crowd of others, at a sporting event or the cinema? Why do you? Or if you always avoid crowds, why do you?

R Do I like crowds? No, not much. I can understand the feelings of fun and tribal loyalty that a crowd of football fans enjoy. But, to me, they seem unpredictable. I prefer arguing in small groups, not shouting out loud assertions of loyalty with thousands of others.

In modern society most of us live in huge groups. We're a 'mass' and we consume 'mass media'. We're a crowd. Both Kierkegaard and Friedrich Nietzsche (1844–1900) were highly critical of crowds. People in crowds relinquish their autonomy as individuals and can be horribly aggressive and violent. Psychologists and philosophers have dutifully investigated and pronounced on crowd behaviour because totalitarian dictators are so adept at manipulating people in crowds. Both Hitler and Stalin used spectacle to arouse emotions – huge crowds, music, banners, shows of military might and so on.

So what happens to individuals in crowds? They feel more anonymous. They surrender their personal responsibilities and have a deep feeling of belonging. They become very emotional, almost hysterical. They feel free to express feelings of panic, joy and anger, sometimes directed against minority groups or 'outsiders'. Skilful orators can encourage individuals to internalize stereotypes.

CASE STUDY German citizens under the sway of Nazism came to believe that German Jews were inferior and part of a huge conspiracy to undermine the country. But everyone at the Nazi rallies knew that Jewish dressmakers, shopkeepers and doctors were just ordinary people trying to get by, like themselves. So what's going on? How did they believe two ideas at the same time? Some psychologists believe that the beliefs of individuals can become 'contaminated' by the presence of large numbers of others.

Most people prefer to adapt to others. Adolescents wear the same clothes, listen to the same music, talk in similar ways. And adults do too – they like to share their beliefs, especially if they're of the same age, economic group, religion, educational background or gender. People like to be liked, they fear rejection and isolation, they often masquerade as one thing in public but think differently at home. But as time wears on, their public mask takes over their private face.

Obeying orders

'Sheeple' are those individuals who accept authority too readily. This may be one of the worst things about us – we're too ready to obey.

The infamous Milgram experiments of the 1960s were designed by psychologist Stanley Milgram to show that this *wasn't* true of freedom-loving American citizens – they wouldn't obey too readily. Individual volunteers were asked to administer electric shocks to students when they got answers wrong in an intelligence test. In fact, the 'students' were just actors and there was no electric shock. The volunteers could hear the 'students' screaming with pain, but over half carried on increasing the voltage up to lethal amounts. Why? Why did ordinary decent Americans do this? Because they were *obeying* the orders of 'scientists' in white coats. It's a salutary lesson to all of us. Never accept orders from others, however powerful, especially if those orders go against your own moral beliefs.

Q Many people prefer to be told what to do. Do you? Or do you always argue about things? Do you do this because you insist on making your own mind up about everything, or are there other reasons?

R Do I want to be told what to think and do? It all depends. If it's expertise about practical matters like plumbing, then I welcome being told what to think and do. If it's moral or political instruction that's being offered, then I resist and argue, as a matter of principle.

The worst kind of collective self-deception is always political. Germany in the 1920s and 30s suffered from economic meltdown and political confusion. A large number of decent German people voted for the National Socialist or Nazi party, which was a bunch of violent, racist and authoritarian thugs. So what's going on here? What caused this massive self-deception among ordinary individuals?

One philosopher and psychologist who thought he knew the answer was Erich Fromm (1900–80). He was born in Frankfurt, where he trained as a psychoanalyst. He fled Nazi Germany in 1934 and spent the rest of his life in America. His most famous book, *The Fear of Freedom*, was published in 1941. Fromm tried to explain why it was that so many decent Germans voted in a horrendous Nazi dictatorship. He thought it was because many people *don't like to be free.*

The political freedoms we now take for granted are quite recent. In medieval societies, everyone knew their place. They had traditional, unchangeable roles. 'I'm a blacksmith, like my father and grandfather. I'm poor but I know where I am and where I belong. There's no real economic competition. So I'm poor, but I won't starve. The church tells me what to believe.' Then capitalism arrived. 'And now I'm free to choose where to live and work. I'm a free individual in a marketplace. There are few shared values any more. I no longer know what to believe. I'm on my own, competing against others for a living. I've lost any sense of direction or meaning in my life. It's frightening. I feel anxious all the time. I don't want all this freedom.'

Escape from freedom

This may be why ordinary people vote for authoritarian governments – because they promise to remove uncertainty and doubt. No one has to choose any more. Everyone is told what to think, so they feel more secure. The government eliminates unorthodox ideas. Books are burnt, and then people. And no one has to make free moral and political decisions any more. This seems to be the worst kind of self-deception. Many German citizens claimed that they had no idea what their Nazi government was doing, which is really a confession that they were wilfully blind to what was going on.

Q a) Governments are usually trying to do the best they can in difficult circumstances; b) Governments are wicked – they tell lies all the time; never trust them. Which of these two views do you have the most sympathy for, and why?

R Are governments wicked or not? I think it's wise to be sceptical but not cynical. Always ask politicians for proof, logical arguments, precise definitions. We all like the warm sound of the 'Big Society'. But what does it actually mean? Politicians are splendidly adept in their use of rhetoric – language used to persuade – so they must always be pinned down to specifics. Sometimes governments do act for the best, in the interests of all of us. But sometimes they don't. This book began with the rule that we must always think for ourselves. That hasn't changed.

Conclusion

So how do we prevent this kind of collective self-deception? Erich Fromm says we need to face up to the fact that we're free individuals, *and* that we must relate to others. We must value *all* of humanity and everyone's freedom. We all have a deep need to belong, but nowadays we value individuality as well. So everyone should think of themselves as unique, with their own free thoughts. Everyone should be 'creative' by determining their own goals. We have to resist all kinds of propaganda and persuasion. Only we ourselves can give our lives meaning. At the same time we should feel that we're part of a community. It's a difficult balance to strike between independence and belonging. But it's one we need to strive for if we're going to flourish as good examples of modern humanity.

Individuals, not sheeple.

---

18. Change

Things change. Nothing stays the same for ever. Don't rely on the world to be the same tomorrow as it was today. Even rocks and stones are changing, slowly. Nothing in this world is fixed or reliable. No life is immune from change.

This is what the ancient Greek philosopher Heraclitus (c. 500 BC) said. He also said no one can step into the same river twice – by the time you wade in for a second time, the water has moved on down to the sea. If Heraclitus were alive he would be astonished. How can we live in a world that changes so unbelievably fast? We're assailed by 24-hour instant news, rushed to us from all corners of the globe. Astonishing electronic devices connect us with all that's happening, everywhere. Information is available at the caress of a touch-sensitive screen. We can travel from here to there at unbelievable heights and at ridiculous speeds. Caught in the middle of all this, we have to try to remain sane and find islands of peace and happiness.

Q How many technological devices do you own, and which do you think you could do without?

R I don't have *that* many gadgets. I'm writing this on a primitive computer. I was given an MP3 player that I can't get to work. I have a mobile phone in the car for emergencies. I still use a video recorder to save TV programmes. I listen to music on cassettes. So I do have a fair number of gadgets, but they're way out of date, like me. Which gadgets could I do without? I wouldn't like to have to write books on a typewriter any more. But I don't really need a mobile phone. I could do without kitchen gadgets like a garlic press and a breadmaker. I prefer gadgets that reduce drudgery but don't interfere with my life too much, like lawnmowers and screwdrivers.

Q Do you think your life is richer and more fulfilled because of gadgets, or do you think that they get in the way?

R If something new appears on the market I'm intrigued but detached. I suspect an iPad would clutter up my life and not liberate me. I still prefer letters to emails. What's the point of Twitter?

Adapt and be ready

Most of us have adapted to a world of accelerated change and, in theory, this should make us more able to cope with changes in our own lives. When we're young, it's easier. When we grow older, it gets harder. We become used to our jobs, partners, friends, homes, and everything else that's reassuringly stable and familiar. If we're fortunate, we change slowly and hardly notice it, except when we take a close look at the mirror. So it's easy to forget that Heraclitan mantra – things change. But sooner or later we will be faced with a sudden massive change – a partner dies, we get a redundancy notice, our health is threatened.

Q Do you take changes in your stride or do they take a long time to come to terms with?

R Some changes to your life seem impossible to deal with – like the death of parents and friends. Events like these will take months or even years to get over. They will visit you again, and return you unexpectedly to feelings of intense grief, guilt and shock. But these feelings will gradually fade into gentle sadness. Life *does* go on.

At first, change can be quite shocking, especially if it's forced upon us out of the blue. Change is the opposite of routine, which is a rather dull substitute for living. But when change comes we often cling on to what we know in a desperate attempt to avoid it or ignore it.

 The secret of survival is usually to go with it, talk about it with others, avoid trying to deal with change all at once, look for what might be good about it, stay cheerful and eventually accept it. People in the past have always had to cope with drastic changes and they've survived. Look at your own life and think of all the other changes you've coped with – more than you might think.

Rousseau thought that change was what made us unique as a species. My cat's 'culture' is hard-wired and has always been the same, for all cats throughout time. But human beings have always changed. Adapting to change and changing ourselves is what makes us different. So it's wise to be ready to adapt to change. The philosopher Epictetus (c. 55–135 AD) said that one obvious way of doing this is to recognize the fragility of human life. If we're unwise and think of our life as something unalterably permanent, when change happens we'll be horribly shocked. We should also live our lives moderately and rationally. We have to acknowledge that nothing lasts for ever, and live our lives facing this fact without being dominated by it. Change is normal. If we face up to that, then we should be able to make a better job at coping with it. We should take Socrates' advice and examine our lives and work out what our priorities are. Should we work less and devote more time to our families and our health? If the answer is no, then at least we see how ambitious and driven we are, and admit that only we are responsible for our lives.

Q Why is it, do you think, that some people cope better with change than others? What do they have that others don't?

R Sometimes it's obvious – they're younger, and more flexible. The philosopher Nietzsche said: 'That which does not kill me, makes me strong' – those who have already experienced some major changes to their lives may be able to cope with one more. Some people are less imaginative than others, and just 'get on'. There's no easy answer to this. Ask people who have survived major life upheavals intact. They might have some very good advice.

Keep it simple

Not all philosophers are critical of frenzied activity, but most are. Plato looked back with envy at a golden age of simplicity that his fellow Athenians had long since abandoned. He thought that to be content meant to avoid unnecessary complexity. He's probably right. It's unwise to be a slave to gadgets that promise to make your life more efficient. Computers were supposed to save time, but actually they steal it from us – keeping up with emails and Facebook. Communicating in cyberspace is a poor substitute for talking to your friends face to face. Technology can make us less human. So remove clutter from your life. Be ruthless with all that stuff.

 Try to organize your life more sensibly so that you have more time to yourself. Think for yourself more. Are your values and beliefs truly your own? If they are, why do you believe in them? If they aren't, well, think hard about where they came from and how you acquired them. It's a good idea to try a bit of rational thought now and again. Don't drift through life without asking questions. Perhaps you should re-examine your relationships with other people and think about how they have changed. Is your work rewarding and interesting? Do you want to be more creative in some way? Are you happy or miserable? What can you do to enhance your life to make it less awful? You probably have more choices than you'd like to admit.

The bad stuff

Sometimes change can be pretty grim. People get ill, they die. How do we cope with that? Most philosophers would say that we just have to be stoical.

Stoicism was a Hellenistic philosophy that flourished during the times of the Alexandrian and Roman empires. Life then was exceptionally hard. Much worse than it is now. We have sophisticated dentistry and anaesthetics. Human beings then were constantly subject to plagues, wars and arbitrary political authority. The Stoics recommended that everyone cultivate soldierly virtues like self-discipline and courage if they were to face up to the hazards of life. They agreed that life can be shockingly hard at times, but thought that it was wise always to have a clear understanding of what it is wise to fear and wise to ignore. They were fatalists, to some extent. There's little or nothing we can do to stop bad things happening, like disease, earthquakes, and the death of loved ones, but it's possible to control our emotions and thoughts. We have to be rational and brave. We have to accept that human life is short and death inevitable, and face these stern facts with courage and tranquility. The Stoics insisted that their philosophy was a way of life, not just an academic pastime. The Roman emperor Marcus Aurelius (121–180 AD) was a practising Stoic who meditated daily on the virtues of wisdom, justice, courage and moderation, and cultivated a kind of tranquil acceptance of the vicissitudes of life. But no one, not even the Stoics, thought life was easy. Some contemporaries of the Stoics called them 'men of stone'. So don't beat yourself up too much if you find change hard to deal with sometimes.

Keep calm and carry on – this is what the Stoics tell us. They were more used to death and dying than we are. Modern society is ill at ease with death and we're more frightened by it too. But most of us survive the death of someone close to us. It can take a long time. You begin by feeling shocked and angry. You may try to deny what has happened. Intense sadness will catch you unawares at different times. You will have sleepless nights. You may feel guilty about what you should have done but didn't. It's wise to distract yourself with routine jobs and plenty of physical exercise. Time will make the feelings less powerful, but it won't take away your memories. You will be a different person, sadder and wiser. Life will go on.

Q What advice would you give to someone else who had to endure a disastrous change to their life? (Divorce, death of a parent or partner, loss of a job, serious illness.)

R When you face a major change in your life, then it's time to call in a few favours from your friends. They must sit there while you pour out your feelings, and try to help you recover. Go for long walks. Get as much sleep as possible. Distract yourself with Scandinavian detective novels. Be as brave as you can, under the circumstances. In a few months' time, your life will improve.

Unfortunately, it's not just everyone else who dies. It's me and you as well, eventually. So how do we cope with that? Religions of various kinds reassure us with tales of reincarnation or everlasting life. Philosophers give us arguments and reasons instead. Anyone who has studied philosophy knows about the death of Socrates. He was accused of corrupting young people (by getting them to think for themselves, probably) and condemned to death by drinking hemlock. He spent his last hours talking away cheerfully about knowledge, the soul, immortality and all good things. Everyone must share what they know, he said, so that, in the end, goodness will triumph. He thought that the best things in life are logic, analysis and friends. Being human means always questions, questions, even if there are no obvious answers. He died bravely and cheerfully, Plato said. The manner of Socrates' death influenced many philosophers, especially the Stoics. They produced many arguments to prove that death is nothing to fear. Here are a few:

- The universe is a rational and harmonious system with a life of its own. And we are a part of that. So, be rational, think for yourself and stay calm. You will be 'returning' to something rather wonderful. This should help you to cope with the fact of your own individual mortality.
- The worst thing about death is probably our fear of it. Conquer this fear and the fact of personal mortality should appear less bleak.
- No one worries about the fact that they didn't exist before they were born, so why worry about the time after death? None of us fears sleep. So why fear death? It's just a sleep from which no one awakes.
- Try to avoid being dominated by thoughts of the past or the future. Nostalgia can make you a prisoner of what's gone, so that you devalue your life now. Don't fear the future. We all live in the present. So be happy with that, and enjoy it as much as you can.

Well, I'm sort of convinced. Today, anyway.

This is what the German philosopher Martin Heidegger (1889–1976) said. He's famous for his extraordinary and impenetrable book – *Being and Time*. What it says, in a very complicated way, is that Being *is* Time. We live in time, and our being ends in death. Being conscious of that fact means that only *we* can give our lives meaning, no one else. This is more or less what Montaigne (1533–92) – one of the more readable philosophers – also said. We will always have the taste of death in our mouths, he thought. We're human, but this can make us forget that we're also animals. Our existence on this planet is limited. This fact should make us humble, and make us brave, so that we can endure the biggest change of all.

IF YOU REMEMBER ONE THING Life means change.

---

19. Meaning? What meaning?

When someone asks what it means to be a good person, at the back of their mind they're also asking about something even more fundamental – **what is the meaning of my life**? The philosopher Schopenhauer thought that one look at the vastness of the heavens made all human life seem utterly insignificant. But it's too easy to use cosmic perspectives like this to diminish the importance of our lives. The universe is impossibly big, but that doesn't make our lives meaningless. We aren't masters of the universe, but that doesn't mean our lives have no value. We're like all natural things in the world: we've evolved, and here we are. We're also fantastically unique, proud and still asking questions, however unanswerable.

A weird question

What is the meaning of life? Some modern philosophers say that asking about the 'meaning' or 'purpose' of life is pointless, empty, or just silly. Meaning is something that we usually associate with language, or some kind of sign system – not with natural things. No one would ask what the meaning of a carrot is. And the word 'life' in this context presumably applies to every human being's existence, in the past, now and in the future – it's a lot of very different lives.

THINK ABOUT IT 'Life' is a very convenient general word that looks as if it's referring to this 'one thing' that all human lives have in common, whereas it's really just pointing to lots of ideas and things that relate to each other in a rather vague sort of way.

The philosopher Ludwig Wittgenstein (1889–1951) thought that, however brilliant and all-inclusive our scientific knowledge becomes in the distant future, this sort of existential question will always remain unanswered. It's intrinsically unanswerable. But this will never stop ordinary people from asking it, especially nowadays. There are some pretty obvious reasons for this, the main one being the general decline of religion that once provided 'answers'. People don't all share the same communal spiritual values and aspirations they once did. We're more reluctant to accept supernatural explanations or consolatory narratives from authority figures. We think we should be able to make up our own minds. We're free to debate ideas and buy small books about them. And neither of us, writer or reader, has to fear the wrath of powerful ecclesiastical authorities any more.

What is the answer?

So what do we know? We know that cooperative behaviour and being kind to others is good for everyone. Others then trust you and like you. They help you survive in a harsh world where vulnerability can be ruthlessly punished. This is why we condemn selfishness and praise sympathy, generosity and kindness. Although not many of us think of strangers as 'family' towards whom we have clear moral obligations, nevertheless we know that it's usually sensible to err on the side of generosity and sympathy in our dealings with them, especially if we're likely to encounter them again.

But that's not really answering these questions: Why be good? Why am I here?

REMEMBER THIS!!! Wittgenstein famously made a very good point about philosophy. He said: 'It leaves the world as it is.' Philosophy helps to clarify questions about being in the world, but it can't provide any final answers. It looks as if it's pointless to ask about the one big thing that gives every individual's life meaning. **Life isn't meaningful or meaningless either. It just doesn't seem to be something that can be discussed in those terms.** It's something we have to get on with, the best we can.

So what have the philosophers taught us?

Aristotle seems to be right: most people thrive best in smaller communities. The scale of modern city life can be horribly alienating as well as fascinating and exciting. But in large cities, neighbours often don't know each other and feel no obligation towards their local districts. City dwellers often don't feel that they 'belong'. All of us feel powerless. We obey autocratic and remote corporations and governments without any sense of commitment. Community spirit is diminished so that individuals feel loyal only to their close families, and little else. We, who are instinctively social and cooperative beings, are not flourishing.

So we should try to foster small groups like teams, clubs, self-help societies and other local organizations. Huge cities, large governments and impersonal corporations may not be good for us, unless they are divided up and somehow made more 'local'. Human beings undoubtedly thrive when they feel embedded in a particular social world of friends and fellow citizens. We need other people if we are to exercise our virtues of trust, reciprocity and solidarity. There *is* such a thing as society and we need it. Those Victorian Utilitarians knew that the more 'public goods' there were, like schools, libraries, parks and local festivals, the more individuals would be able to fulfil their shared *and* individual lives.

Finding a middle way

John Stuart Mill realized that striking a balance between the individual and the community is difficult. Small communities can be traditionalist, reactionary and suspicious of individual eccentricity. The tyranny of majority opinion can be oppressive. So every individual should feel that they belong but also feel free to pursue different sorts of lifestyles and interests, however odd they may appear to others.

THINK ABOUT IT

Everyone is an eccentric to someone else. We must leave people alone and allow them to flourish in all sorts of different ways, provided no is harmed. In a modern pluralist society, full of different people all seeking their own ways of living, we are allowed to tut tut at – but must tolerate – mad poets, rash mountain-climbers, tree-worshippers, and rebellious teenagers. That way society won't stagnate, and it's usually more fun.

Heidegger reminded us that we're forever pushed forward in time. We have to spend our lives in a perpetual present, but we can't help both remembering our past and imagining what our futures will be. Our attitude to time will depend on how old we are. When we're young, we search for meaningful work and satisfying relationships and projects for the future. But you're only young once, so enjoy it while you can. When we're older, it's easy to become trapped in an idealized past life that, we convince ourselves, had more meaning to it than life does now. Harmless nostalgia can give rise to a reactionary dislike of all things new, and young people in general.

REMEMBER THIS!!!

We have to be nice to the young, because we need them. Modern society is a dynamic project that rushes forward into a new and confusing future. We need young people to help us understand it.

The future but not as we know it

Aristotle recommended we have reasonable expectations from life, recognize it for what it is, and know that it can never be perfect. So we shouldn't go through life pretending we will never die. But nor should we lead desperate and restless lives constantly trying to accumulate as many disparate experiences as possible.

 The trick is to walk down the middle path between total denial and fearful fixation.

Heidegger reminded us that we're the only beings who know about the inevitability of our own deaths. We're always 'thrown' into the future, that place where we're going to live tomorrow and the next day. Because of this we need to plan and be ready to meet all sorts of challenges. But beware. Kierkegaard warned us that a life that involves the endless postponement of happiness for an imagined life of future bliss is usually a wasted life.

This is where Sartre advises and admonishes us:

- We have to think things out for ourselves. Only we can decide what to do with our lives.

- We shouldn't rely on other people, ideologies, fate or inertia to control our lives or decide who we are.
- The goals that our modern society currently tries to force upon us are mostly trivial and ultimately unsatisfying. We're consumers, but that's not *all* we are.

We may not be as free as Sartre thinks we are, but perhaps we should act as if we were. A healthy scepticism may not be such a bad thing. Keep asking questions. We all have to make compromises in order to eat regular meals and sleep in a warm, dry bed. But there's still more to life than shopping malls.

The radiant future

Socialists, anarchists and other Utopianists once promised us that, one day, we would reach that golden city on the hill where all hard work and money are abolished. But not many of us think that capitalism will disappear tomorrow. It may get moulded into something more humane, egalitarian, ecological and stable. We and our children are going to have to learn how to live with it but not let it dominate and delineate our lives. We have to make it our servant and not our master.

The Epicureans thought that most people are at their happiest and most fulfilled when they live in a community. They themselves would argue and debate all day long in their beautiful gardens. And they knew that only *you* can decide on the meaning of *your* life. We have to live as authentically and as happily as we can. Most of us need some kind of commitment and feelings of achievement for our lives to seem worthwhile. This usually involves fulfilling work, loving relationships, maybe some kind of spirituality.

THINK ABOUT IT Sartre thought that you should be creative about your life – think of it as like writing a novel or building a house that you will never finish.

The end

Compared to the giant tortoise's average of 177 years, human life is short. Things always change. So be prepared to adapt. Fortunately, human beings are usually pretty good at that. The universe is indeed very, very big and sometimes scary, but the earth is very beautiful and not a bad place to be, provided we look after it better.

So let's be like the Stoics. Remain confident and sensible. Be brave and resolute in adversity, because some days will undoubtedly be bad, or even awful.

Help those who are unfortunate, because you'll probably need them to come to your aid one day. Eat plenty of fresh fruit and vegetables. Take lots of exercise. Learn to play a musical instrument. Keep an open mind. Be adventurous but not foolhardy. Read lots. Join a reading group. Learn a foreign language. Appreciate what you can achieve. Everybody can learn how to draw. Believe in what you want, but try not to proselytize too much. Have a positive attitude to life. It's better to be a disappointed optimist than a smug pessimist. Save energy and recycle. There's still only one planet. Be a good neighbour and a loyal friend.

There it is. We got there. How to be a good person.

 IF YOU REMEMBER ONE THING Only you can decide.

Bibliography

There are hundreds and hundreds of books that tell you how to live your life. Some of them are great. A lot are awful. This is a book fashioned by philosophical ideas, so most of the books here are 'philosophical'.

Introductions to morality

What is Good? by A.C. Grayling (Phoenix, 2004) is a very readable introduction to this puzzling question about how we should behave and what we should try to become. He's quite hostile to religious answers, though.

The Origins of Virtue by Matt Ridley (Penguin, 1997) is a very readable account of why and how we humans have gone in for morality.

Introducing Ethics: A Graphic Guide by Dave Robinson and Chris Garratt (Icon Books, 2008) is a light-hearted survey of the history of moral philosophy, with cartoons.

Practical Ethics by Peter Singer (Cambridge University Press, 1979) examines and discusses many of the usual topics like abortion and euthanasia. Singer is an enthusiastic Utilitarian.

A Companion to Ethics, ed. Peter Singer (Blackwell, 1991) is a hefty but mostly readable tome on many of the key subjects and problems of ethical philosophy.

Readers will have noticed that the philosopher **Aristotle** appears frequently in this book. His most famous work on ethics and flourishing is: *Nicomachean Ethics*, Aristotle (Penguin, 1998).

Two books about Aristotle are: *Introducing Aristotle* by Rupert Woodfin and Judy Groves (Icon Books, 2001); and *Aristotle on the Perfect Life* by Anthony Kenny (Clarendon Press, 1996).

Everyone should read: *The Last Days of Socrates*, Plato (Penguin, 1969).

The Trial of Socrates by I.F. Stone (Picador, 1989) is a re-examination of Socrates the man and the reasons why he was condemned to death by a democratic government.

The Republic by Plato (Penguin, 1955) is very readable. The first third of the book is full of vigorous and interesting debates. After that, it's the blueprint for a 'perfect' and rather odd society.

Books on unorthodox religions and spirituality

Mysticism: A Study and an Anthology by F.C. Happold (Pelican, 1963).

The Varieties of Religious Experience by William James (Longmans, 1952).

Religion and Morality: Essays, ed. G. Outka and J.P. Reeder (Doubleday, 1973).

Books about human nature

Leviathan by Thomas Hobbes (Everyman, 1914) is a
   powerful indictment of the wickedness of human
   nature and the corresponding need for strong
   government.
The Social Contract by Jean-Jacques Rousseau (Everyman,
   1930) is Rousseau's attempt to retrieve naturally good
   men from a wicked society.
Existentialism and Humanism by Jean-Paul Sartre, trans.
   Philip Mairet (Methuen, 1973) is a readable and short
   explanation of how and why we must 'make ourselves'.
No one has ever accused **Kant** of being an easy read,
   but *The Moral Law*, trans. H.J. Paton (Hutchinson,
   1953) isn't too much of a slog. You might be better
   off reading one or two books on Kantian ethics first,
   though, like *The Categorical Imperative*, by H.J. Paton
   (Hutchinson, 1947).

The major writings of the **Utilitarians** are more accessible,
but no one has ever called Bentham an entertaining writer:
An Introduction to the Principles of Morals and Legislation
   by Jeremy Bentham (Athlone Press, 1970)
Utilitarianism by J.S. Mill (Collins, 1962).

And you could also read:
Utilitarianism, For and Against by J.J.C. Smart and B.
   Williams (Cambridge, 1973).

If you're interested in **virtue theory**, then you should read
   After Virtue by A. MacIntyre (University of Notre Dame
   Press, 1981).

There are many books about friendship, romantic love, marriage, parenting, moral development, business, consumers,
citizenship, environmentalism, self-deception, creativity,
change and the 'meaning' of life. Here are just a few:

The Essays of Montaigne (Penguin, 1991) (the essay 'On
   Friendship')

Friendship: A Philosophical Reader, ed. N.K. Badhwar
   (Cornell University Press, 1993)

Sexual Desire by Roger Scruton (Free Press, 1986)

Marriage – A History by S. Coontz (Penguin, 2006)

The Rights of Women by Mary Wollstonecraft (Penguin,
   1997)

Children, Rights and Childhood by D. Archard (Routledge,
   2004)

Parents and Children: The Ethics of the Family by J.
   Blustein (Oxford University Press, 1982)

Clones, Genes and Immortality by J. Harris (Oxford
   University Press, 1998)

Essays on Moral Development by L. Kohlberg (Harper &
   Row, 1981)

Public and Private Morality, ed. S. Hampshire (Cambridge
   University Press, 1978)

The Theory of the Leisure Classes by Thorstein Veblen
   (Dover, 1994)

Affluenza by Oliver James (Vermilion, 2007)

Status Anxiety by Alain de Botton (Hamish Hamilton, 2004)

Introducing Political Philosophy by Dave Robinson and Judy Groves (Icon Books, 2008)

On Liberty by J.S. Mill (Oxford University Press, 1991)

The Life You Can Save by Peter Singer (Random House, 2009)

Animal Liberation by Peter Singer (Random House, 1990)

A Companion to Environmental Philosophy, ed. D. Jamieson (Blackwell, 2001)

Seeing Through Self-Deception by A. Barnes (Cambridge University Press, 1997)

The Fear of Freedom by Erich Fromm (Routledge, 2001)

Hellenistic Philosophy by A.A. Long (Duckworth, 1996)

What's It All About? by Julian Baggini (Granta, 2008)

On the Meaning of Life by J. Cottingham (Routledge, 2003)

The Meaning of Life by Terry Eagleton (Oxford University Press, 2007).

Index